William A. Kaplin

Barbara A. Lee

The Supplement to
A Legal Guide for Student Affairs Professionals, Second Edition

JOSSEY-BASS
A Wiley Imprint
www.josseybass.com

Published by Jossey-Bass
A Wiley Imprint
989 Market Street, San Francisco, CA 94103-1741—www.josseybass.com

Jossey-Bass books and products are available through most bookstores. To contact Jossey-Bass directly call our Customer Care Department within the U.S. at 800-956-7739, outside the U.S. at 317-572-3986, or fax 317-572-4002.

Jossey-Bass also publishes its books in a variety of electronic formats. Some content that appears in print may not be available in electronic books.

The Supplement to A Legal Guide for Student Affairs Professionals, 2nd Edition,
ISBN: 978-1-118-03187-2

Library of Congress Cataloging-in-Publication Data
Kaplin, William A.
    A legal guide for student affairs professionals / William A. Kaplin, Barbara A. Lee.
    — 2nd ed.
      p. cm.
    Includes bibliographical references and index.
    ISBN 978-0-470-43393-5 (alk. paper)
      1. College students—Legal status, laws, etc.—United States. 2. Universities and colleges—Law and legislation—United States. I. Lee, Barbara A. II. Title.
    KF4243.K36 2009
    344.73'079—dc22

                                       2008049095

Printed in the United States of America

FIRST EDITION

PB Printing   10 9 8 7 6 5 4 3 2 1

Notice of Web Site and Periodic Supplements

The authors, in cooperation with the publisher, have made arrangements for two types of periodic updates for the second edition of *A Legal Guide for Student Affairs Professionals* (*SA 2d*). First, the authors prepare periodic supplements to *SA 2d* (as they also do for *The Law of Higher Education*, fourth edition (*LHE 4*) and the *Student Version* of *LHE 4*). This 2011 *Supplement* is the first such supplement for *SA 2d*. Second, the National Association of College and University Attorneys (NACUA) hosts a Web site for *SA 2d* (as well as for *LHE 4* and the *Student Version*), the primary purpose of which is to provide quick access to the authors' brief updates and citations on major new developments and resources that affect the discussions in these books. The Web site may be accessed through the NACUA Web site at http://www.nacua.org/publications/lohe. Further directions for using this Web site are also available at this address.

Both of these updating services for users of *A Legal Guide for Student Affairs Professionals,* second edition, are intended to be a response to the law's dynamism—to the rapid and frequent change that occurs as courts, legislatures, government agencies, and private organizations develop new requirements, revise or eliminate old requirements, and devise new ways to regulate and influence institutions of higher education.

The authors have not designed *SA 2d* to be used as a teaching text in college courses. For instructors who do wish to use the book for that purpose, however, there are two sets of teaching materials on the authors' NACUA Web site that may be of assistance. One set is keyed to *LHE 4*; the other set is keyed to the student edition (*Student Version*) of *LHE 4*. By perusing the tables of contents for these teaching materials, instructors should easily be able to identify edited cases, notes and questions, problems, and large-scale problem exercises that could be used in conjunction with *SA 2d*.

Contents

Preface

This volume updates and supplements *A Legal Guide for Student Affairs Professionals,* second edition, 2009 (hereafter *SA 2d*), published by Jossey-Bass, Inc., Publishers. The 2011 *Supplement* covers developments from the press deadline for *SA 2d* in mid-2008 through December, 2010. We have included discussions of court opinions, statutes, regulations, and related developments, as well as bibliography entries and text cites to selected law journal articles, books, Web sites, and other new resources. In selecting new developments for inclusion, we have considered, primarily, the development's significance for higher education; the development's fit with the subject matter and themes of *SA 2d;* and the development's usefulness for filling in gaps, clarifying, or updating specific points in *SA 2d.* When selecting cases, we have also considered the completeness and helpfulness of the reasoning in the court's opinion.

The 2011 *Supplement* is organized to parallel *SA 2d.* Each new development is keyed to a particular section of *SA 2d.* Occasionally, other entries are also included in particular sections under the heading Clarification or the heading Erratum. If the development modifies or extends a specific point in *SA 2d,* a page reference is also provided in parentheses: for example, "(see *SA 2d,* p. 247)." Similarly, whenever a development can be better understood with reference to some background material in *SA 2d,* a reference to the pertinent page or section of *SA 2d* is provided in parentheses. Internal cross-references to other sections of this *Supplement* are also used as appropriate: for example, "(see this *Supplement,* Section 4.3)."

In addition to providing further development of issues discussed in *SA 2d,* we have also added new issues and developments. Topics receiving the most extensive treatment include the ruling of the U.S. Supreme Court on the application of institutions' nondiscrimination policies to faith-based student organizations (*Christian Legal Society v. Martinez*); the continuing struggle to balance the requirements of the free exercise and establishment clauses of the First Amendment in regard to state funds for sectarian institutions or their students; attempts of students to claim that institutions and their faculty have a fiduciary duty with respect to their interactions with students; implications of new laws such as the 2008 amendments to the Americans with Disabilities Act, the Lily Ledbetter Pay Equity Act, and the Genetic Information Nondiscrimination Act (GINA); developments in interpretations of Fourth Amendment protections against searches of both students and employees at public institutions; and the continuing impact on academic freedom of the U.S. Supreme Court's decision in *Garcetti*, in which the Court ruled that public employees are not protected by the First Amendment if their speech is work-related. In addition, this *Supplement* examines new developments in sexual harassment law (of and by both students and faculty, as well as third parties); new requirements imposed by the Higher Education Opportunity Act of 2008; student protest and lawful institutional restrictions on such activities; student academic freedom in the context of course and clinical requirements; and other student free speech and press issues. In order to account for new developments not treated extensively in *SA 2d*, we have added three new subsections: coaches' contracts (Section 4.2.3), the rights of transgender employees (Section 4.5.2.8), and state gun possession laws and their implications for institutions' policies against weapons on campus (Section 13.2.7).

Earlier versions of much of the material in this *Supplement* previously appeared on our Web site for *SA 2d* and our related publications, hosted by the National Association of College and University Attorneys. *SA 2d* material posted on the Web site prior to December 31, 2010 was removed shortly after publication of this *Supplement*. We will still update this Web site, however, with *SA 2d* developments occurring after December 31, 2010, as well as with occasional clarifications and errata. The Web site may be accessed at www.nacua.org/publications/lohe/index.asp. For the *SA 2d* postings, look under Additional Resources for *A Legal Guide for Student Affairs Professionals*. We will continue to make such postings for *SA 2d* on our Web site until publication of the next supplement.

As with *SA 2d* (see p. xxii), the 2011 *Supplement* is not intended as a substitute for the advice of legal counsel. Nor, in a problem-solving context, is it intended as a substitute for research into the primary legal resources or for individualized study of each legal problem's specific circumstances.

August 2011
William A. Kaplin   Washington, DC
Barbara A. Lee   New Brunswick, N.J.

Acknowledgments

The authors extend their appreciation to Jossey-Bass, Inc., publisher of *A Legal Guide for Student Affairs Professionals*, 2nd edition (*SA 2d*), for its cooperation in the publication of this 2011 *Supplement*. We also appreciate the support of the National Association of College and University Attorneys (NACUA), which graciously sponsors a Web page on which we posted updates to *SA 2d* from the time of its publication (as well as updates to the fourth edition of *The Law of Higher Education* and the *Student Version* of the fourth edition of *The Law of Higher Education*).

We are also grateful to the persons who assisted us in various ways with the preparation of the manuscript. Taylor Stevens, Sarah Grimme, and Andrew Garcia, former students at Stetson University College of Law, assisted with the research. Donna Snyder, at The Catholic University of America School of Law, provided important organizational and word processing services, as did Louise Petren and her staff at Stetson. Dean Veryl Miles at Catholic law school provided a summer research grant to W.K. to support work on this *Supplement*; and Dean Darby Dickerson at Stetson supported W.K.'s work on the *Supplement* in various important ways. B.L. is grateful to Rutgers University for approving a sabbatical leave that provided time to prepare this *Supplement* and other scholarly work.

NACUA has encouraged and supported our work for many years. We are grateful to Kathleen Curry Santora and Karl Brevitz for their consistent support, and for their willingness to create and manage the special *Law of Higher Education* Web site that we use to keep all of our books up-to-date and to provide resources for instructors who use either the fourth edition, the *Student Version*, or *SA 2d*. Linda Henderson, formerly manager of publications for NACUA, was instrumental in creating and updating the Web site, and we continue to appreciate, and benefit from, her professional assistance and moral support. Jen Morrissey, NACUA's program specialist, has ensured that all of our Web-based updates were posted in a timely fashion.

We also appreciate the patience and understanding of our families, who have supported our work over the decades, and who clearly understand the dynamism of higher education law and its importance to the various constituencies that we serve.

About the Authors

William A. Kaplin is research professor of law at The Catholic University of America, Washington, D.C., where he is also special counsel to the university general counsel. He is also Distinguished Professorial Lecturer at the Stetson University College of Law in Florida and a Senior Fellow of Stetson's Center for Excellence in Higher Education Law and Policy. He has been a visiting professor at Cornell Law School, at Wake Forest University School of Law, and at Stetson; a distinguished visiting scholar at the Institute for Higher Education Law and Governance, University of Houston; and a visiting scholar at the Institute for Educational Leadership, George Washington University. He is a former editor of *The Journal of College and University Law*, and now serves as a member of its editorial board. He is a former member of the Education Appeal Board at the U.S. Department of Education. He is also a member of the U.S./U.K. Higher Education Law Roundtable that had its first meeting in summer 2004 at New College, Oxford University, and a mentor/leader for the bi-annual Higher Education Law Roundtable for emerging scholars at the University of Houston Law Center.

Professor Kaplin received the American Council on Education's Borden Award, in recognition of the first edition of *The Law of Higher Education*, and the Association for Student Judicial Affairs' D. Parker Young Award in recognition of research contributions. He has also been named a Fellow of the National Association of College and University Attorneys.

In addition to coauthoring the fourth edition of *The Law of Higher Education*, Professor Kaplin has also coauthored (with Barbara A. Lee) *The Law of Higher Education, Fourth Edition: Student Version* (Jossey-Bass, 2007); *Cases, Problems, and Materials for Use with The Law of Higher Education* (NACUA, 2006); and *A Legal Guide for Student Affairs Professionals,* second edition (Jossey-Bass,

2009). He also authored *American Constitutional Law: An Overview, Analysis, and Integration* (Carolina Academic Press, 2004).

William Kaplin received his B.A. degree (1964) in political science from the University of Rochester and his J.D. degree *with distinction* (1967) from Cornell University, where he was editor-in-chief of the *Cornell Law Review*. He then worked at a Washington, D.C. law firm, served as a judicial clerk at the U.S. Court of Appeals for the District of Columbia Circuit, and was an attorney in the education division of the U.S. Department of Health, Education and Welfare before joining the Catholic University law faculty.

****

Barbara A. Lee is professor of human resource management at the School of Management and Labor Relations, Rutgers University, in New Brunswick, N.J. She is also of counsel to the law firm of Edwards Angell Palmer & Dodge, LLP. She is a former dean of the School of Management and Labor Relations, and also served as associate provost, department chair, and director of the Center for Women and Work at Rutgers University. She chaired the editorial board of the *Journal of College and University Law*, served as a member of the Board of Directors of the National Association of College and University Attorneys, and was named a NACUA Fellow. She was elected to membership in the American Law Institute (ALI), serves on the executive committee of the New Jersey State Bar Association's Section on Labor and Employment Law, and formerly served on the executive committee of the Human Resource Management Division of the Academy of Management. Professor Lee is the immediate past chair of the Higher Education Committee of the New Jersey State Bar Association. She is also a member of the U.S./U.K. Higher Education Law Roundtable. She received a distinguished alumni award from the University of Vermont in 2003, the Daniel Gorenstein Award from Rutgers University in 2009, and the William A. Kaplin Award for Excellence in Higher Education Law and Policy Scholarship from Stetson University College of Law in 2010.

In addition to coauthoring the third and fourth editions of *The Law of Higher Education*, their supplements and updates, the derivative work *A Legal Guide for Student Affairs Professionals* (1997), and the supplementary teaching materials, *Cases, Problems, and Materials,* Professor Lee also coauthored *Academics in Court* (1987, with George LaNoue), and has written numerous articles, chapters, and monographs on legal aspects of academic employment. She serves as an expert witness in tenure, dismissal, and discrimination cases, and is a frequent lecturer and trainer for academic and corporate audiences.

Barbara Lee received her B.A. degree, *summa cum laude* (1971) in English and French from the University of Vermont. She received an M.A. degree (1972) in English and a Ph.D. (1977) in higher education administration from The Ohio State University. She earned a J.D., *cum laude* (1982) from the Georgetown University Law Center. Prior to joining Rutgers University in 1982, she held professional positions with the U.S. Department of Education and the Carnegie Foundation for the Advancement of Teaching.

1

Overview of
Higher Education Law

Sec. 1.3. The Governance of Higher Education

1.3.1. Basic concepts and distinctions. In recent years, momentum has been building for modifications in state governance structures that would facilitate collaboration between higher education and K–12 education on issues of mutual concern, such as improving high school students' preparation for college. New types of entities, developed for this purpose, are generally grouped under the title "K–16 initiatives" or "P–16 initiatives." These initiatives may be attached to the state governor's executive offices or to the statewide public university system, or may be set up as a separate state-level commission or council. See, e.g., "Diplomas Count 2008: School to College: Can State P–16 Councils Ease the Transition?" (*Education Week,* June 5, 2008), available at http://www.edweek.org/ew/articles/2008/06/05; Peter Schmidt, "A Tough Task for the States: Efforts to Get Schools and Colleges to Cooperate Yield Both Fixes and Frustration," *Chronicle of Higher Education,* p. B6 (March 10, 2006). Collaboration between higher education and K–12 education, and modification of state governance structures to accommodate such collaboration, become increasingly important as the interdependencies and mutuality of interests between K–12 and higher education become increasingly clear. See generally William Kaplin, *Equity, Accountability, and Governance: Three Pressing Mutual Concerns of Higher Education and Elementary/Secondary Education,* IHELG Monograph 06–11 (Institute for Higher Education Law and Governance, Univ. of Houston, 2007).

1.3.3. External governance. In recent years there has been considerable discussion concerning new concepts of the "public" university and potential new state governance models to fit these new concepts. Decreased state

1

oversight of (and thus increased autonomy for) public universities, decreased state funding, and the consequent appearance of "privatization" have been prominent focal points of the debate. See, for example, Katherine Lyall & Kathleen Sell, *The True Genius of America at Risk: Are We Losing Our Public Universities to DeFacto Privatization?* (Praeger, 2005); Christopher Newfield, *Unmaking the Public University: Forty-Year Assault on the Middle Class* (Harvard Univ. Press, 2008).

Sec. 1.4. Sources of Higher Education Law

1.4.2. External sources of law

1.4.2.5. Foreign and international law. Advances in communication and easy access to digital documents have exposed faculty and college administrators to new legal issues, including issues involving the laws of other nations. For example, a German court entered an injunction requested by six academic publishers against a file-sharing company, RapidShare AG, which had been giving away digital versions of scholarly books, a copyright violation. Steve Kolowich, "A Win for Publishers." *Inside Higher Education*, February 24, 2010, available at http://www.insidehighered.com/news/2010/02/24/publishers.

In another incident, a New York University law professor was charged with libel in France on the basis of a book review, written by a law professor in France, that the NYU professor posted on a Web site affiliated with a law journal for which that professor is the editor. The journal is a joint partnership between NYU and the Academy of European Law. The plaintiff is a professor at a business school in Israel. Aisha Labi, "NYU Professor Faces Libel Lawsuit in France for Refusing to Purge Negative Book Review." *Chronicle of Higher Education*, February 25, 2010, available at http://chronicle.com/article/NYU-Professor-Faces-Libel-L/64370/. And academics have been sued for libel in British courts because British law requires plaintiffs to prove only that they "have a reputation to defend" in the UK and that the allegedly defamatory material was circulated in the UK, which, if it were posted on a Web site, would not be difficult to prove. Jon Ungoed-Thomas and Michael Gillard, "Libel Tourists Flock to 'Easy' UK Courts," *Sunday Times(UK)*, November 1, 2009, available at http://timesonline.co.uk/tol/news/uk/articles6898172.ece.

Sec. 1.5. The Public-Private Dichotomy

1.5.2. The state action doctrine. *Husain v. Springer*, 494 F. 3d 108 (2d. Cir. 2007), provides another example of state action issues concerning students. A Student Government Publications Commissioner at a public university impounded copies of an issue of the student newspaper, and certain members of the student senate had supported this action. These students were among the defendants in a First Amendment suit brought by the newspaper editors and other students (see entry on *Husain v. Springer* in sec. 10.3.3. below). The student defendants argued that they had not engaged in state action and therefore should be dismissed from the case. The district court and the appellate court agreed. The college did not compel or require the student defendants to impound the newspaper, nor did the college encourage this action. To the contrary, the college president had overruled the student government's action. Moreover, even it could be said that college regulations and policies provided authorization for the students to act, "state authorization was insufficient to establish that the student government defendants were state actors in the circumstances presented here." (For a contrary case, in which a court held student government members to be engaged in state action, see *Amidon v. Student Ass'n of the State Univ. of New York at Albany*, 399 F. Supp. 2d 136 (N.D.N.Y. 2005).)

Another case, *Limpuangthip v. United States*, 932 A. 2d 1137 (D.C. 2007), provides an example of state action issues concerning employees. A private university's search of a student's room had led to the student's conviction on drug charges, and the student argued that the search was state action violating the Fourth Amendment. The search had been conducted by a university administrator accompanied by two university police officers. The administrator was concededly a private actor, not subject to the Fourth Amendment, but the police officers, although employees of the university, were Special Police Officers (SPOs) under District of Columbia law, "authorized to exercise arrest powers broader than that of ordinary citizens and security guards." The student claimed that this governmental authority of the SPOs present at the search made the search state action. The appellate court agreed that SPOs do become state actors when they invoke their state authority "through manner, word, or deed," this is, when they act "like . . . regular police officer[s]" rather than employees of a private entity. But the two SPOs, according to the court, did not act in this manner at the search. The administrator had initiated and conducted the search herself; the SPOs had not influenced the administrator's actions; and their "involvement in the search was peripheral." Their conduct therefore "does not amount to state action." (For another state action case about private university police officers who are SPOs, see *Maniaci v. Georgetown University* in Section 7.3.1 of this *Supplement*.)

Sec. 1.6. Religion and the Public-Private Dichotomy

1.6.3. Government support for religious institutions. The case of *Colorado Christian University v. Weaver*, 534 F.3d 1245 (10th Cir. 2008), provides further perspective on both institutional-based aid and student-based aid programs, and on some of the key cases, in particular *Locke v. Davey* (*SA 2d*, pp. 43–45), *Mitchell v. Helms* (*SA 2d*, pp. 41–42), and *Roemer v. Board of Public Works* (4th Cir., 2001) (*SA 2d*, pp. 40–41).

Colorado Christian University (CCU), an evangelical, nondenominational institution, was one of two schools whose students were denied participation in state-operated scholarship programs. The pertinent state statutes provided that scholarships were available to eligible students who attend any accredited college in the state, other than colleges that the state determines to be "pervasively sectarian." The government purpose for the law was "awarding scholarships to deserving students as universally as federal law permits." The Colorado legislature had added the "pervasively sectarian" language to ensure that the scholarship programs met the federal establishment clause requirement, articulated by the Supreme Court in *Roemer v. Board of Public Works*, 426 U.S. 736, 755 (1976), "that no state aid at all [may] go to institutions that are so 'pervasively sectarian' that secular activities cannot be separated from sectarian ones" (citing *Hunt v. McNair*, 413 U.S. 734 (1973)).

CCU challenged the "persuasively sectarian" exclusion on various grounds under the establishment clause, the free exercise clause, and the equal protection clause. Explaining that all three of these clauses apply to religious discrimination, the Tenth Circuit gave prominence to the establishment clause in its analysis but emphasized that "the requirements of the Free Exercise Clause and Equal Protection Clause proceed along similar lines." Ultimately, the court ruled in CCU's favor, holding the exclusion to be unconstitutional for two reasons: it "expressly discriminates among religions without constitutional justification, and its criteria for doing so involve unconstitutionally intrusive scrutiny of religious belief and practice."

Based on the parties' joint stipulation of facts, the court gave this description of the pervasively sectarian exclusion:

> To be eligible for any of the scholarship programs, a student must attend an "institution of higher education." Colo. Rev. Stat. §§23–3.5–102(2), 3.3–101(2), 3.7–102(3), 18–102(5)(a)(I).
>
> The state statutes defining such an institution exclude any college that is "pervasively sectarian" as a matter of state law. *Id.* §§3.5–102(3)(b), 3.3–101(3)(d), 3.7–102(3)(f), 18–102(9). As to the meaning of this term, the statutes provide:
>
> (1) An institution of higher education shall be deemed not to be pervasively sectarian if it meets the following criteria:
>
> (a) The faculty and students are not exclusively of one religious persuasion.
>
> (b) There is no required attendance at religious convocations or services.
>
> (c) There is a strong commitment to principles of academic freedom.
>
> (d) There are no required courses in religion or theology that tend to indoctrinate or proselytize.
>
> (e) The governing board does not reflect nor is the membership limited to persons of any particular religion.
>
> (f) Funds do not come primarily or predominantly from sources advocating a particular religion. *Id.* §§23–3.5–105, 3.3–101(3)(d), 3.7–104. [534 F.3d at 1250–51.]

Although the Colorado legislature had inserted these provisions into the aid program statutes in order to comply with the U.S. Supreme Court's establishment clause law (see above), the law had changed since the statutes were enacted. The court made clear that the "parties agree that under current inter-pretation, the Establishment Clause poses no bar to inclusion of CCU in the Colorado scholarship programs." The Colorado legislature had not, however, repealed its statutory restriction on "pervasively sectarian" institutions.

The court framed the issue arising from these facts as follows:

> It is now settled that the Establishment Clause permits evenhanded funding of education—religious and secular—through student scholarships. . . . It is therefore undisputed that federal law does not *require* Colorado to discriminate against Colorado Christian University in its funding programs. Rather, the parties' dispute centers on whether the State may nonetheless choose to exclude pervasively sectarian institutions, as defined by Colorado law, even when not required to. [534 F.3d at 1253.]

Ruling for the plaintiff CCU, the court answered this question in the negative.

The state defendants had argued that this case was controlled by *Locke v. Davey*, 540 U.S. 712 (2004) (*SA 2d*, pp. 43–45). The court agreed that *Locke* did stand for a general proposition that supported the defendants: "the Free Exercise Clause does not mandate the inclusion of religious institutions within every government program where their inclusion would be permissible under the Establishment Clause" (534 F.3d at 1254). But the court also determined that the specifics of the *CCU* case were distinguishable from *Locke* in ways that precluded *Locke* from being controlling:

> [T]he Colorado ["pervasively sectarian"] exclusion, in addition to imposing a far greater burden on affected students, has two features that were not present in *Locke* and that offend longstanding constitutional principles: (1) the Colorado exclusion expressly discriminates *among* religions, allowing aid to "sectarian" but not "pervasively sectarian" institutions, and it does so on the basis of criteria that entail intrusive governmental judgments regarding matters of religious belief and practice. . . . (2) *Locke* involved neither discrimination among religions nor intrusive determinations regarding contested religious questions. The scholarship program at issue in *Locke* excluded all devotional theology majors equally—without regard to how "sectarian" state officials perceived them to be—and therefore did not discriminate among or within religions. *Locke*, 540 U.S. at 715–16. Evangelicals and Unitarians, Catholics and Orthodox Jews, narrow sectarians and freewheeling latitudinarians, all were under the same interdiction. And since under the program "[t]he institution, rather than the State, determine[d] whether the student's major [was] devotional," the State did not engage in intrusive religious inquiry. *Id.* at 717. [534 F.3d at 1256 (numbering added).]

These distinctions, as explained and emphasized by the court in *CCU*, provide helpful guidelines regarding the inclusion of religious institutions, religious programs of study, and religious students within governmental programs of financial aid.

Focusing on the first distinction above (the Colorado exclusion expressly discriminates among religions), the court emphasized that the "neutral treatment of religions . . . without discrimination or preference" is a clear command of both the establishment clause and the free exercise clause. In contrast, according to the court, the Colorado exclusion serves "to exclude some but not all religious institutions" from participation in state student aid programs. This is "discrimination 'on the basis of religious views or religious status'" (quoting *Employment Division v. Smith*, 494 U.S. at 877). The "discrimination is expressly based on the degree of religiosity of the institution and the extent to which that religiosity affects its operations, as defined by such things as the content of its curriculum and the religious composition of its governing board." The Colorado exclusion therefore violated the basic religious neutrality principle inherent in the establishment and free exercise clauses.

Focusing on the second distinction above (the Colorado exclusion involves intrusive governmental judgments on matters of religious belief and practice), the court began with the basic principle that government may not make eligibility decisions concerning religious institutions based on "intrusive judgments regarding contested questions of religious belief or practice." This principle, the court explained, typically is associated with the establishment clause's "prohibition of 'excessive entanglement' between religion and government," which "protects religious institutions from governmental monitoring or second-guessing of their religious beliefs and practices, whether as a condition to receiving benefits . . . or as a basis for regulation or exclusion from benefits [as in this case]." The Colorado exclusion provision was "fraught with entanglement problems." All six of the criteria for determining pervasive sectarianism (see above) presented such problems. According to the court, the "most potentially intrusive" of the six criteria is (1)(d), which requires the staff of the Colorado Commission on Higher Education "to decide whether any theology courses required by the university 'tend to indoctrinate or proselytize.'" As applied in this case, this criterion foments excessive entanglement:

> Commission officials testified that they demanded to see CCU's religious education curriculum, and (for reasons known only to themselves) determined that it "tend[ed] to indoctrinate or proselytize." The line drawn by the Colorado statute, between "indoctrination" and mere education, is highly subjective and susceptible to abuse. [534 F.3d at 1262.]

The "indoctrination" criterion, along with the other five, thus violated the "intrusive judgments" principle above. Government may not make eligibility decisions regarding religious institutions based on such subjective and contested criteria. Rather, if government chooses to distinguish among religious institutions, "it must employ neutral, objective criteria rather than criteria that involve the evaluation of contested religious questions and practices."

Since the state had no weighty governmental interests that could justify the two types of religious discrimination embodied in Colorado's statutory provisions on the pervasively sectarian exclusion, the court invalidated these provisions.

1.6.4. Religious autonomy rights of individuals in public postsecondary institutions.
A 2005 case provides an instructive example of institutional activities other than group prayer that may raise establishment clause issues. The case, *O'Connor v. Washburn University*, 416 F.3d 1216 (10th Cir. 2005), also illustrates the type of establishment claim premised on institutional disapproval of or hostility to religion rather than institutional *endorsement* of or *support* for religion. In both respects, the case serves to extend the discussion in the main text.

In *O'Connor*, a professor and a student claimed that the university (a public university) had installed a statue on campus that negatively and offensively portrays Roman Catholicism, thus violating their establishment clause rights. According to the appellate court, the statue, "entitled 'Holier Than Thou,' depicts a Roman Catholic Bishop with a contorted facial expression and a miter that some have interpreted as a stylized representation of a phallus." The statue had been selected along with four others, in an annual competition, "for displaying in a temporary outdoor sculpture exhibition [that] supplements the university's collection of twenty-five [permanent] outdoor statues." Selection of the five temporary statues was made by a three-person jury of art professionals chosen by the university's Campus Beautification Committee, and both the committee and the university president had approved the selections. Once the statue was installed along a "high traffic sidewalk," the university began receiving numerous complaints from within and outside the university. The university considered the complaints but declined to remove the statue.

In ruling on the establishment clause claim, the appellate court applied the *Lemon* test (see *SA 2d*, pp. 46, 48), as modified by the "endorsement or disapproval" test (see 416 F.3d at 1223–24), placing more emphasis on the latter test (often called just the "endorsement test") than did the courts in the cases discussed in the main texts. The endorsement test focuses on whether the governmental activity at issue "has either (1) the purpose or (2) the effect of conveying a message that religion or a particular religious belief is favored or preferred, on the one hand, or disapproved or disparaged on the other. Under the first, "purpose," prong of the test, the question is "'whether' the government's actual purpose is to endorse or disapprove of religion." Under the second, "effect," prong, the question is "whether a reasonable observer aware of the history and context of the [activity at issue] would find the [activity] had the effect of favoring or disfavoring a certain religion [or religious belief]." (See 415 F.3d at 1227–31, quoting *Bauchman ex rel. Bauchman v. W. High School*, 132 F.3d at 551–52.) Applying this test, the court focused on whether, in the context of all the pertinent facts, the university's selection or placement of the statue, or its refusal to remove it after receiving complaints, had "either (1) the purpose or (2) the effect of conveying a message" that the university disapproved of or disparaged Roman Catholicism or a particular Catholic belief.

Regarding "purpose," the court determined that the plaintiffs had not produced any evidence that the university's actions were motivated by a disapproval of Catholicism, and that the university had other aesthetic and educational "reasons" for its decisions. Regarding "effect," the court determined that, even if the effect of the statue was to convey "an anti-Catholic message" (a point on which the court did not rule), a "reasonable observer viewing [the statue] in context would understand that the university had not approved or agreed with that message."

It was important to the court's reasoning that the "Holier Than Thou" statue was displayed on a university campus rather than, say, in a city park or on the grounds of a county office building. The court emphasized that a campus is "peculiarly the marketplace of ideas" (citing *Healy v. James*, 408 U.S. at 180), a place where government "acts against a background and tradition" of academic freedom (citing *Rosenberger v. Rector & Visitors of Univ. of Va.*, 515 U.S. at 835). Moreover, the placement and retention of the statue, in context, had implicated the university's educational mission and its curriculum. Even though the statue was not created as part of a course, it was nevertheless "part of [the university's] educational curriculum"; the president and the vice president of academic affairs had both "testified that they strove to extend the educational environment . . . beyond the classroom to encompass various stimuli including art, theatre, music, debate, athletics, and other activities."

Apparently, in such academic, higher education contexts, courts may accord public colleges and universities more leeway than other governmental entities to establish religiously neutral educational reasons for engaging in activities that involve religion in some way. Similarly, in this context, courts may find it less likely that a reasonable observer "would associate" a particular, allegedly religious, message with the college or university itself (416 F.3d at 1229–30). More broadly, these attributes of higher education serve to support the assertion, made by the U.S. Supreme Court and repeated by lower courts, "that religious themes 'may constitutionally be used in an appropriate study of history, civilization, ethics, comparative religion, or the like'" (416 F.3d at 1230, quoting *Stone v. Graham*, 449 U.S. 39, 42 (1980)).

* * * *

A recent U.S. Supreme Court case, *Pleasant Grove City v. Summum* (2009), introduces an additional dimension to cases like *O'Connor v. Washburn University* (*SA 2d*, pp. 47–49). *O'Connor* was an establishment clause challenge to a governmental entity's placement of religious monuments or statues on public property. *Pleasant Grove*, in contrast, illustrates how there could also be free speech clause challenges to such practices. Faced with such a challenge, according to the Court, the governmental entity may often prevail by characterizing the placement of the monument or statue as "governmental speech" rather than "private speech." Success with this argument, however, would not insulate the governmental entity from an establishment clause challenge, which requires a separate analysis.

Selected Annotated Bibliography

Sec. 1.1. *(How Far the Law Reaches and How Loud It Speaks)*

Brown, Deborah, Przypyszny, John, & Tromble, Katherine (eds.). *Legal Issues in Distance Education: A Legal Compendium* (Nat'l Ass'n of College & Univ. Attys., 2007). A comprehensive compendium addressing a variety of issues, including accreditation and state and federal regulation; copyright, intellectual property, and other technology issues; discrimination and accessibility-related issues for individuals with disabilities; and student affairs, and academic and disciplinary misconduct, in the context of distance education.

Wildavsky, Ben. *The Great Brain Race: How Global Universities Are Reshaping the World* (Princeton Univ. Press, 2010). Characterizes higher education as a form of "international trade," citing the mobility of students and faculty members, competition among institutions of higher education globally for top students, and the sharp increase in the number of international campuses created by U.S. colleges and universities; includes examples from Saudi Arabia, China, and India of new or expanded universities attempting to function on a global level.

Sec. 1.2. *(Evolution of Higher Education Law)*

Hacker, Andrew, & Dreifus, Claudia. *Higher Education? How Colleges Are Wasting Our Money and Failing Our Kids* (Times Books, 2010). A controversial and critical analysis of the cost and benefits of higher education, with suggestions on improving educational quality and reducing its cost.

Lee, Barbara A. "Fifty Years of Higher Education Law: Turning the Kaleidoscope." 36 *J. of Coll. & Univ. Law* 649 (2010). Reviews the expansion of the regulation of higher education and identifies ten areas of change that have affected the practice of higher education law over the past fifty years.

O'Neil, Robert. *Academic Freedom in the Wired World: Political Extremism, Corporate Power, and the University* (Harvard U. Press, 2008) (see description in *Selected Annotated Bibliography* for Chap. 7, section 7.1, of this *Supplement*).

Tierney, William, & Hentschke, Guilbert. *New Players, Different Game: Understanding the Rise of For-Profit Colleges and Universities* (Johns Hopkins, 2007). Addresses the origins and growth of for-profit higher education and the potential impacts of for-profit education on traditional, nonprofit higher education and on higher education policy and governance. Compares the strengths and weaknesses of for-profit versus nonprofit colleges and universities.

Sec. 1.6. *(Religion and the Public-Private Dichotomy)*

Schuman, Samuel. *Religious Colleges in Twenty-First-Century America* (Johns Hopkins Press, 2009). Reviews the history of early religiously affiliated colleges, examines three Roman Catholic institutions, and profiles evangelical colleges and universities. Using interviews with administrators, faculty, and students, the author explores the challenges and goals of these institutions.

2

Legal Planning and Dispute Resolution

Sec. 2.2. Litigation in the Courts

2.2.3. Judicial (academic) deference. A Georgia state appellate court has ruled that "disputes concerning academic decisions made by public institutions of learning present no justiciable controversy," and that a trial court's injunction requiring a university to reinstate a student was erroneously awarded. In *Board of Regents of University System of Georgia v. Houston*, 638 S.E. 2d 750 (Ga. Ct. App. 2006), a student who was suspended for two semesters after he was arrested for attempting to arrange a marijuana sale sought a temporary restraining order to reinstate him at Georgia Institute of Technology (Georgia Tech) and to the football team. Despite the fact that the discipline was for social (and criminal) misconduct rather than for academic misconduct, the court, quoting earlier decisions by the Georgia Supreme Court, applied the academic abstention doctrine to the case. Said the court, "Absent plain necessity impelled by a deprivation of major proportion, the hand of the judicial branch alike must be withheld," citing *McDaniel v. Thomas*, 285 S.E.2d 156 (1981). The court explained that the student had not raised equal protection claims, and stated that "there is no right to participate in extracurricular sports, including football." Therefore, the trial court lacked jurisdiction over the controversy.

For a thoughtful and thorough analysis of the evolution and, perhaps, the weakening of the academic deference doctrine, see Robert M. O'Neil, "Judicial Deference to Academic Decisions: An Outmoded Concept?" 36 *J. Coll. & Univ. Law* 729 (2010).

Sec. 2.4. Institutional Management of Liability Risk

2.4.1. Overview and suggestions. The tragic effects of Hurricane Katrina on New Orleans and its higher education institutions have served to cast a spotlight on the intricacies of property insurance and its role in institutional risk management. A group of cases consolidated under the title *In Re: Katrina Canal Breaches Litigation* provides a striking example. The cases were all suits against insurance companies that had refused to pay claims for property damages resulting from Katrina and the failure of the New Orleans levees. One of the plaintiffs was Xavier University, which alleged that it had suffered damages in excess of $30 million and sought recovery under its commercial, "all-risk," property insurance policy (*Xavier University of Louisiana v. Travelers Property Casualty Co. of America*, 495 F.3d 191 (5th Cir. 2007)).

In the *Xavier* case and the other cases consolidated with it, the insurance companies argued that damages caused by "flood" were specifically excluded from the plaintiffs' policies. The plaintiffs argued "that the massive inundation of water into the city was the result of the negligent design, construction, and maintenance of the levees and that the policies' flood exclusions in this context are ambiguous because they do not clearly exclude coverage for an inundation of water induced by negligence." In a complex opinion, the federal appellate court drew upon the law regarding insurance contracts, rules for construing contract terms, cases on flood exclusion clauses, other cases on water damage claims, and various sources containing definitions of "flood." On this basis, the court rejected the plaintiffs' arguments:

> [W]e conclude that the flood exclusions are unambiguous in the context of this case and that what occurred here fits squarely within the generally prevailing meaning of the term "flood." When a body of water overflows its normal boundaries and inundates an area of land that is normally dry, the event is a flood. This is precisely what occurred in New Orleans in the aftermath of Hurricane Katrina.
> . . . . That a levee's failure is due to its negligent design, construction, or maintenance does not change the character of the water escaping through the levee's breach; the waters are still floodwaters, and the result is a flood. [495 F.3d at 221.]

(In the concluding part of the opinion, the court also addressed technical matters concerning the "doctrine of efficient proximate cause," relied on by the plaintiffs, and the "anti-concurrent-causation clauses" in many of the insurance policies at issue, concluding that the doctrine, and the clauses, did not apply to the case (495 F.3d at 221–23)).

Selected Annotated Bibliography

Sec. 2.4. (Institutional Management of Liability Risk)

Novak, Kimberly J., & Lee, Art M. *Student Risk Management in Higher Education: A Legal Compendium.* (Nat'l Assn. of College & Univ. Attys., 2007). A collection of law review articles, reports, conference presentations, policies, forms, and other materials related to reducing the risk of liability in student affairs matters. Topics addressed include student travel and transportation, residential life, student organizations, events involving minors, athletic events, sports clubs, alcohol and other drugs, high risk behavior and mental health issues, and academic internships and externships.

3

The College and Its Trustees

Sec. 3.1. The Question of Authority

3.1.1. Overview. Trustees of both public and private colleges and universities have a fiduciary duty to act in the best interests of the institution and to avoid conflicts of interest. A consent judgment involving Stevens Institute of Technology requires substantial changes in the way its board of trustees operates. The consent judgment was entered in January of 2010 to settle a lawsuit brought by the New Jersey Attorney General against the president and several board members. The lawsuit alleged that the president's salary and benefits were excessive, that the board chair and president had withheld important information from the rest of the board concerning spending and borrowing by the institution, and that other board members had withheld from the rest of the board a report that indicated that the institution's internal accounting controls were inadequate.

The consent judgment requires substantial changes in board governance, including term limits for board members, a requirement that the entire board, rather than a committee or an individual board member, approve the compensation of the president and the other five most highly paid employees, review financial information at each board meeting, meet with the external auditor annually, review the performance of the endowment annually, and conduct annual evaluations of board members. The consent judgment also requires that the board engage independent consultants to make recommendations on best practices for the audit committee, and sets term limits for both trustees and faculty on board committees.

The consent judgment provides a blueprint for good board governance practices.

3.1.2. Trustee authority. The attorney general of Kentucky issued an advisory opinion stating that the governing board of the Kentucky Community

Technical College System did not have the authority to change the tenure system for newly hired faculty. In the spring of 2009, the board voted to cease the practice of awarding tenure to faculty hired after July 1, 2009 and to use a system of renewable term contracts. The attorney general determined that the board's decision conflicted with state tenure laws, and thus the board was not authorized to eliminate tenure, even for newly hired faculty. Opinion OAG09–08 (September 21, 2009).

Sec. 3.2. *Institutional Tort Liability*

3.2.1. *Overview.* A New Jersey appellate court applied the doctrine of charitable immunity (*SA 2d*, p. 111) to shield Fairleigh Dickinson University from liability for the death of a student. In *Orzech v. Fairleigh Dickinson University*, 985 A.2d 189 (N.J. Super., App. Div., 2009), the appellate court reversed the ruling of the trial court that charitable immunity did not apply in this case because the student, a residence hall advisor, had consumed a substantial amount of alcohol and thus was not a "beneficiary" of the educational institution's "charitable objectives," nor was the university engaging in charitable works when it allegedly allowed parties involving the consumption of alcohol by students in residence halls. A jury had found the student and the university equally negligent, and the university appealed.

The court determined that "a student, while living in a dormitory (whether or not also an RA) is receiving the benefits of the school's educational works," and thus the university was protected by charitable immunity. It ruled that neither the university's alleged negligence in failing to enforce its alcohol policy, nor the student's alleged negligence in consuming too much alcohol and falling out of a window in his residence hall room, negated the charitable immunity doctrine or negated the fact that the student was a beneficiary of the university.

3.2.2. *Negligence.* Is property owned by a university but used for faculty housing part of the "campus" such as to create a duty to "invitees" who are injured on that property? A state appellate court has refused to award summary judgment in a case involving these issues. In *Clark Atlanta University v. Williams*, 654 S.E.2d 402 (Ga. Ct. App. 2007), a student at a nearby institution, Morris Brown College, had been on Clark Atlanta's campus for a program which he was eligible to attend because his college is part of a consortium in which Clark Atlanta participates. The student, Williams, was leaving the campus and stopped to chat with friends on the lawn of a faculty home that is owned by Clark Atlanta. He was robbed and shot by two individuals while on that property, which is across the street from the residence hall in which Williams lived.

Williams sued Clark Atlanta for negligence, arguing that it had a duty of ordinary care because it owned the land on which he was injured. The court ruled that a jury must decide whether the property on which Williams was injured was part of Clark Atlanta's campus and if so, whether Williams lost his status as an invitee after he left the program he was attending. The court ruled that the sole issue to be resolved at trial was whether Clark Atlanta had a duty of ordinary care, which requires a jury to determine whether or not Williams was an invitee at the time of his injury.

3.2.2.4. Liability for cocurricular and social activities. A federal appellate court has ruled that staff of Paul Smith College did not have a duty to protect a student from injuries sustained in a snowmobile accident. The college is located on a lake, and because the lake is not owned by the college, students had a practice of building bonfires on the frozen lake and using it as a location for consuming alcohol. A student and his guest had consumed considerable alcohol and went for a snowmobile ride around the lake. The snowmobile crashed and the two were killed. The guest was twenty years old.

In *Guest v. Hansen*, 603 F.3d 15 (2d Cir. 2010), the student's guest's father sued Paul Smith College and its director of residence life for negligence because they knew that students were consuming alcohol and partying on the frozen lake and they neither attempted to stop the party nor enforced the college's alcohol policy. The court affirmed the trial court's ruling that neither the college nor the director of residence life owed the decedents a duty of care because they were not on property controlled by the college. Even if the college had the ability to control the off-campus activities of its students and their guests, said the court, it had no obligation to do so.

3.2.2.5. Student suicide. A federal trial court refused to dismiss a series of claims brought against Dominican College by the plaintiff after her daughter, a student at the college, committed suicide following a sexual assault on campus. In *McGrath v. Dominican College of Blauvelt, New York*, 672 F. Supp. 2d 477 (S.D.N.Y. 2009), the mother brought claims under Title IX and Section 1983, as well as common law tort claims of fraud, intentional infliction of emotional distress, negligence, and wrongful death, alleging that the college's inappropriate and insufficient response to the student's complaint was a direct cause of her suicide.

Because this matter was before the court on the defendants' motion to dismiss, and no trial had been held, the court relied on the plaintiff's allegations in order to make its ruling. The plaintiff alleged that the college had failed to properly investigate a previous sexual assault against another student because it had referred that victim to a local police officer who was also an instructor at the college. After the plaintiff's daughter was sexually assaulted in her residence hall room by three men after consuming alcohol at a residence hall party (a violation of college policy), she reported the assault to the appropriate college personnel, and they referred her to the same police officer, but allegedly did not inform her of other campus procedures for filing assault complaints. Although the student and her mother met with the dean of students, the plaintiff alleged that he discouraged them from filing campus charges, told them to wait for the results of the criminal investigation, and told them that the alleged assailants would not be disciplined. No report from the police department was forthcoming, and, according to the plaintiff, despite the student's concern for her safety if she returned for her sophomore year at the college, the college offered no accommodations. The student withdrew from the college and committed suicide at home several months later.

The trial court ruled that a fact finder could conclude that the college was deliberately indifferent to the student's requests for assistance after the assault. It also concluded that the plaintiff had stated a colorable claim of denial of equal protection under Section 1983, despite the fact that the college is private, because it "delegated its investigative responsibilities to the Orangetown Police Department through a police detective who was also an employee of the College." The court also ruled that the fraud and emotional distress claims were adequately supported by allegations to survive the defendants' motion to dismiss.

* * * *

In an unreported opinion, a state trial court denied Wesleyan University's motion for summary judgment in a lawsuit accusing the university of negligence and breach of fiduciary duty as a result of the suicide of a student. In *Leary v. Wesleyan University*, 2009 Conn. Super. LEXIS 621 (Conn. Super. Ct. Middlesex, March 10, 2009), the father of the student asserted that the actions of the university's public safety officers contributed to the student's death. The student had called public safety, stating that he was having a panic attack. The public safety officers picked him up, drove him to a local hospital, and dropped him off there. The student left the hospital shortly thereafter and committed suicide. The father's negligence claim contained allegations that the university had not properly hired or trained its public safety officers, and that because the student's suicide was foreseeable, the officers did not follow the proper procedures in dealing with the student. The university moved for summary judgment.

The court denied summary judgment on the negligence claim because it believed that it was necessary to determine whether or not the student was in the "custody and control" of the public safety officers when they took him to the hospital. If he were, then the court could find that a special relationship existed, which would create a duty to protect the student (citing *Schieszler v. Ferrum College* (see *SA 2d*, p. 124)). The court also rejected the defense's claim that §323 of the Restatement of Torts was inapposite in this case. (That section discusses the duty that is created when an individual undertakes to render services to another which he should recognize as necessary to protect that individual, and provides for liability if those services either increase the harm to the person served or the harm is caused by the person's reliance on the individual who rendered the services.) The court also ruled that whether or not the student's suicide was foreseeable by the public safety officers was not resolved, and would have to be adduced at trial.

The court rejected the plaintiff's attempt to state a claim of breach of fiduciary duty, ruling that the actions of the public safety officers did not involve the type of close relationship and dependence that the doctrine requires. The court awarded summary judgment to the university on that claim.

3.2.3. *Educational malpractice.* Courts continue steadfastly to refuse

to entertain claims by students (or their heirs) that injuries they received, whether physical or financial, were due to educational malpractice. For example, in *Dallas Airmotive, Inc. v. Flightsafety International, Inc.*, 277 S.W.3d 696 (Mo. Ct. App., W.D., 2008), a state appellate court rejected the claims of survivors of a plane crash that the flight school's failure to train the pilot properly resulted in the fatal crash. The appellate court affirmed the trial court's award of summary judgment to the defendants, noting that educational malpractice claims were not cognizable in Missouri on the grounds of the same public policy considerations articulated in earlier cases discussed in *SA 2d*, p. 127.

Sec. 3.4. *Institutional Liability for Violating Federal Constitutional Rights (Section 1983 Liability)*

For an example of a more recent case upholding the Eleventh Amendment immunity of a state university, see *Bowers v. National Collegiate Athletic Association*, 475 F. 3d 524 (3d Cir. 2007), involving the University of Iowa. The Third Circuit now uses the "*Fitchik* factors" (from a prior case of the same name) and applied them in *Bowers*. These factors constitute a "three-part test" that "examines [these] three elements: (1) whether the payment of the judgment would come from the state; (2) what status the [university] has under state law; and (3) what degree of autonomy the [university] has" (475 F. 3d at 546). Each factor is to be given equal weight. Applying the factors in "a fact-intensive review that calls for individualized determination," the court concluded that "the first Fitchik factor weighed slightly against immunity, while the second and third factors weighed heavily in favor of immunity." Accordingly, the court ruled that the University of Iowa falls within the scope of Eleventh Amendment immunity.

Selected Annotated Bibliography

Sec. 3.2. *(Institutional Tort Liability)*

Dickerson, Darby. "Background Checks in the University Admissions Process: An Overview of Legal and Policy Considerations." 34 *J. Coll. & Univ. Law* 420 (2008). Discusses legal and policy issues related to the use of background checks for student admissions.

Dunkle, John H., Silverstein, Zachary B., & Warner, Scott C. "Managing Violent and Other Troubling Students: The Role of Threat Assessment Teams on Campus." 34 *J. Coll. & Univ. Law* 586 (2008). Discusses the use of "threat assessment" teams as a mechanism for preventing violence on campus, including a review of "best practices" and applicable ethical and legal standards [issue 3].

Lake, Peter F. "Still Waiting: The Slow Evolution of the Law in Light of the Ongoing Student Suicide Crisis." 34 *J. Coll. & Univ. Law* 253 (2008). Updates his 2002 article with Nancy Tribbensee (Peter Lake & Nancy Tribbensee, "The Emerging Crisis of

College Student Suicide: Law and Policy Responses to Serious Forms of Self-Inflicted Injury," 32 *Stetson L. Rev.* 125 (2002)) by reviewing subsequent court rulings and discussing the guidance (or lack thereof) by courts concerning institutional duties to at-risk students.

Lee, Barbara A., & Abbey, Gail E. "College and University Students with Mental Disabilities: Legal and Policy Issues." 34 *J. Coll. & Univ. Law* 349 (2008). Reviews protections for students with mental disabilities under the ADA and Section 504 of the Rehabilitation Act. Analyzes student challenges to academic dismissals and discusses judicial deference to academic decision making. Reviews challenges to disciplinary dismissals and the legal rights of at-risk students. Makes a series of suggestions for college and university policy and practice.

Massie, Ann MacLean. "Suicide on Campus: The Appropriate Legal Responsibility of College Personnel." 91 *Marq. L. Rev.* 625 (2008). Argues that institutions must do more to prevent students from self-harm. Proposes a rule under §314A of the Restatement of Torts creating a duty to protect a student from self-harm if college officials have actual knowledge of a previous suicide attempt.

Moore, Heather E. "University Liability When Students Commit Suicide: Expanding the Scope of the Special Relationship." 40 *Ind. L. Rev.* 423 (2007). Discusses the evolution of the special relationship doctrine, focusing on *Shin* and *Schieszler*. Suggests strategies for preventing and responding to suicide attempts.

Peters, Kristen. "Note: Protecting the Millennial College Student." 16 *S. Cal. Rev. L. & Social Justice* 431 (2007). Reviews the efforts of students and their parents to hold colleges increasingly responsible for student safety. Proposes a "Millennial Model" of institutional duty, which would create a per se special relationship based on the "reasonable detrimental reliance" of the millennial generation of college students. An interesting contrast to the Bickel and Lake concept of the college as "facilitator" and consequent theories of liability.

Sokolow, Brent A., Lewis, W. Scott, Keller, James A., & Daley, Audrey. "College and University Liability for Violent Campus Attacks." 34 *J. Coll. & Univ. Law* 319 (2008). Reviews the potential defenses of colleges and universities to lawsuits regarding violent attacks on campus, including lack of foreseeability, lack of duty, and sovereign immunity.

Tribbensee, Nancy. "Privacy and Confidentiality: Balancing Student Rights and Campus Safety." 34 *J. Coll. & Univ. Law* 383 (2008). Reviews the requirements of the Family Educational Rights and Privacy Act (FERPA) and concludes that the law is not a bar to effective prevention activities with respect to at-risk students.

Wei, Marlynn. "College and University Policy and Procedural Responses to Students at Risk of Suicide." 34 *J. Coll. & Univ. Law* 285 (2008). Discusses the interplay between mental health treatment and discipline for students who threaten or attempt suicide. Recommends against discipline and proposes that mediation be used prior to the use of involuntary medical withdrawals or other attempts to exclude the student from campus.

4

The College and Its Employees

Sec. 4.2. Employment Contracts

4.2.3. Coaches' contracts (new section). Employment contracts between the institution and athletics coaches are fertile grounds for litigation. There have been numerous lawsuits, most of which have been settled, involving coaches who either have been dismissed or who have left before the end of the contractual period.

For example, the football coach at Kansas State University was dismissed in 2008 after a losing season. According to press reports, the coach, Ron Prince, had entered a "secret agreement" with the athletics director for additional compensation in the event that he was dismissed. The university sued the former coach to invalidate the agreement, asserting that university officials, with the exception of the athletics director, were unaware of the agreement. Brad Wolverton, "Kansas State Scrambles to Invalidate Secret $3.2 Million Deal Between Ex-Athletics Officials," *Chron. Higher Educ.*, May 20, 2009, available at http://chronicle.com/article/Kansas-State-Scrambles-to-I/47618/. The coach countersued, claiming that university officials were aware of the agreement. Austin Meek, "Ex-coach now seeking punitive damages beyond $3.2 million buyout," *Topeka Capital-Journal*, Aug. 10, 2009, available at http://cjonline. com/sports/football/2009–08–10/prince_seeking_3_million. A trial was scheduled for June of 2011. Other examples include a lawsuit brought by a coach who was dismissed by the University of Kentucky. The case settled. Libby Sander and Paul Fain, "Coaches' Contracts are Fertile Ground for Conflict," *Chron. Higher Educ.*, June 4, 2009, available at http://chronicle.com/article/ Coaches-Contracts-Are Fert/44424/. And West Virginia University sued a football coach for breach of contract, under a buyout provision in his contract, when the coach left for a job at the University of Michigan before his contract had expired. The settlement was for $4 million, part of which the University of Michigan agreed to pay. Paul Fain, "Former Football Coach Agrees to Pay

$4 Million to West Virginia U. *Chron. Higher Educ.,* July 9, 2008, available at http://chronicle.com/article/Former-Football-Coach-Agree/41282/.

Another issue, which may be covered in more coaches' contracts in the future, is the return of performance bonuses paid to coaches if wins are later vacated by the NCAA for rules violations. Dan Wolken, "University of Memphis Fine-Tuning Coaching Contracts," *The Commercial Appeal,* April 9, 2010, available at http://www.commercialappeal.com/news/2010/apr/09/u-of-m-fine-tuning-contracts/.

The importance of carefully drafting coaches' contracts, and anticipating as many issues in advance as possible, was underscored in a case involving Ohio State University. In *O'Brien v. The Ohio State University,* 2006 Ohio 1104, 2006 Ohio 4737 (Ct. Claims Ohio 2006), the plaintiff, who had been the head basketball coach at Ohio State University, was fired after he was determined to have violated NCAA rules in recruiting and providing financial assistance to a player who was not an amateur athlete but a professional. O'Brien alleged that his dismissal breached his contract because his conduct in violating one NCAA rule was not a material breach of the contract. The court agreed, and found that one NCAA rule violation, which the court found to be minor, was not material and thus the termination of the coach's contract was without cause. The court awarded the former coach just under $2.5 million in damages.

Disputes between institutions and their current or former coaches create a "perfect storm" of public relations problems for institutions—especially those that receive public funds. Contracts for coaches should deal with as many foreseeable situations as possible, including disclosure of additional compensation received by the coach, what will happen if wins are negated for NCAA rules violations, who is responsible for payments to the institution should the coach leave before the end of the contract, and under what circumstances the coach will be dismissed.

Sec. 4.3. *Collective Bargaining*

4.3.3. *Collective bargaining and antidiscrimination laws.* The U.S. Supreme Court issued a 5–4 ruling that limits its previous ruling in *Alexander v. Gardner-Denver* (see *SA 2d,* p. 147). In *14 Penn Plaza LLC, et al. v. Pyett,* 129 S. Ct. 1456 (2009), the court ruled that a detailed grievance and arbitration provision in a collective bargaining agreement that specifically included discrimination claims was binding on the individual bargaining unit members, despite its earlier ruling in *Gardner-Denver.* The Court distinguished *Gardner-Denver* from the situation in the *14 Penn Plaza* case. In *14 Penn Plaza,* the grievance and arbitration provision specifically included discrimination claims and had been "freely negotiated" between the union and the multi-employer association, while in *Gardner-Denver,* the issue was whether contract-based discrimination claims were limited to an arbitration forum. Furthermore, said Justice Thomas, writing for the majority, the Court had upheld the lawfulness of arbitration clauses agreed to by employees who were not represented by unions that require that discrimination claims be arbitrated. The result in *14 Penn Plaza* removes the "advantage" that unionized employees previously

enjoyed of being able to process their discrimination claims both through a grievance and arbitration process and through a lawsuit.

* * * *

A federal appellate court has ruled that a union contract provision that requires an employee to choose between arbitrating a grievance and pursing a discrimination charge with the EEOC or in the courts does not violate the law. In *Richardson v. Commission on Human Rights and Opportunities*, 532 F.3d 114 (2d Cir. 2008), the plaintiff had been terminated and filed a grievance with her union. She also filed a claim of race discrimination with the state Commission on Human Rights and Opportunities. The collective bargaining agreement stated that "disputes over claimed unlawful discrimination shall be subject to the grievance procedure but shall not be arbitrable if a complaint is filed with the Commission on Human Rights and Opportunities arising from the same common nucleus of operative fact." Relying on that contract language, the union refused to take the grievance to arbitration. The plaintiff then filed a retaliation claim against the union with the state Commission on Human Rights and Opportunities, as well as with the EEOC.

Although the EEOC determined that the choice of remedies provision in the collective bargaining agreement violated Title VII, the state Human Rights agency and subsequently the trial court disagreed. The court awarded summary judgment to the employer on both the discrimination and retaliation claims, finding that the collective bargaining agreement language allowed the plaintiff to file an EEOC charge and to sue her employer in court; the lack of access to arbitration under the contract did not diminish any of the plaintiff's rights, according to the court. The court distinguished *Gardner-Denver* because it required a plaintiff pursuing a grievance under a collective bargaining agreement to waive his or her right to file an EEOC charge or a lawsuit. The provision in question in this case, said the court, was the opposite in that it allowed a plaintiff to select an administrative or judicial forum for resolution of the dispute rather than arbitration.

Sec. 4.4. *Personal Liability of Employees*

4.4.2. Tort liability. As discussed in *SA 2d*, Sec. 4.4.4, the litigation under Section 1983 between the families of students killed or injured in the Texas A&M bonfire tragedy has ended with the courts' decisions that the university cannot be sued because it is protected by sovereign immunity. Subsequently, the families filed tort claims in state court against both the university and several administrators in their personal capacity. Although the trial and appellate courts agreed that the university itself was protected by sovereign immunity, the trial court permitted the lawsuit against the individual defendants to go forward, and the appellate court affirmed. In *Bowen et al. v. Comstock et al.*, 2008 Tex. App. LEXIS 3927 (Ct. App. Tex. 10th Dist., May 28, 2008), the court ruled that the individual defendants were not protected by sovereign immunity, and that the state court had jurisdiction over these claims. The three-judge panel ruled 2–1 that, despite the fact that the individual defendants may be able to assert defenses of "official immunity" or may be able to demonstrate that they did not have a duty to protect the students from harm, the plaintiffs should have an opportunity to have their claims heard in court. The dissenting judge believed that the claims were actually against the state, not the individuals, and that sovereign immunity should protect them as well.

4.4.4. Constitutional liability (personal liability under Section 1983)

4.4.4.1. Qualified immunity. In *Saucier v. Katz* (*SA 2d*, p. 154), the U.S. Supreme Court had mandated that courts take up the two immunity inquiries (*SA 2d*, p. 154) in the order specified. In *Pearson v. Callahan*, 129 S.Ct. 808 (2009), however, the Court determined that

> while the sequence set forth [in *Saucier*] is often appropriate, it should no longer be regarded as mandatory. The judges of the district courts and the courts of appeals should be permitted to exercise their sound discretion in deciding which of the two prongs of the qualified immunity analysis should be addressed first in light of the circumstances in the particular case at hand [129 S. Ct. at 818]

4.4.4.2. Issues on the merits: State-created dangers.
Clarification. Litigation against Texas A&M University administrators continued in state court, as tort law claims, after dismissal of the federal section 1983 suits discussed in *SA 2d*, pp. 156–158. See Sec. 4.4.2. above, and see also Katherine Mangan, "Texas Court's Ruling in Bonfire Case Opens New Liability Worries for Campuses," *Chron. Higher Educ.* (June 2, 2008). The state court suits have now been settled. See Katherine Mangan, "Texas A&M U. and Former Officials Settle Bonfire Lawsuit for 2.1 Million," *Chron. Higher Educ.* (Oct. 29, 2008); and see also http://tamunews.tamu.edu /bonfirestatement/.

Sec. 4.5. Employment Discrimination

4.5.2. Sources of law

4.5.2.1. Title VII. Claims filed by employees asserting that they were retaliated against for filing discrimination complaints or for simply complaining about alleged workplace discrimination have skyrocketed in the past decade. This expansion occurred as a result of two cases decided by the U.S. Supreme Court—one in 2006, and the other in January of 2009. In 2006, the U.S. Supreme Court ruled that an employee who was transferred to a less desirable job after complaining of discrimination could state a claim for retaliation, even if the new job had the same pay and benefits (*Burlington Northern v. White*, 548 U.S. 53 (2006)). In that case, the Court explained that Title VII's language prohibiting retaliation did not limit the definition of retaliation to compensation or terms and conditions of employment. If the employer's response to a complaint of discrimination was "materially adverse" to an employee—such as changing the work schedule of a single mother such that it made it difficult for her to arrange for child care—such an action could constitute retaliation.

The Court examined the concept of retaliation more recently in *Crawford v. Metropolitan Government of Nashville and Davidson County, Tennessee,* 129 S. Ct. 846 (2009*).* In *Crawford,* a human resources officer of the Metro School District asked Vicky Crawford, who had worked for the school district for thirty years, if she had witnessed any "inappropriate behavior" by Gene Hughes, the school district's employee relations director. Crawford had not reported any harassment, but in response to the request, described several instances of harassing behavior toward her by Hughes. Two other employees also reported being harassed by Hughes. The school district took no action against Hughes, but fired Crawford and the two other employees who had reported harassment. The district asserted that Crawford had been fired for embezzlement, although no charges were filed against her.

Title VII prohibits two forms of retaliation: "opposing a practice made an unlawful practice" (the "opposition clause") and retaliation resulting from the individual's participation "in any manner in an investigation, proceeding, or hearing" (the "participation clause"). Crawford accused the school district of violating both clauses.

The trial court awarded summary judgment to the school district, and the U.S. Court of Appeals for the Sixth Circuit affirmed. Both courts ruled that, because she had not filed a complaint of discrimination, but had merely answered questions during the internal investigation of Hughes' behavior, she had not engaged in behavior meeting the requirements of the opposition clause. And because no charge had been filed with the EEOC, the lower courts ruled that Crawford did not meet the requirements of the "participation" clause. The U.S. Supreme Court rejected that reasoning.

Justice Souter, writing for seven of the nine Justices, found that Crawford's actions satisfied the requirements of the "opposition" clause, even though she had not filed a formal complaint. He noted that an employee may oppose a supervisor's action without taking aggressive action to complain about it or stop it. Crawford's response to the management employee's question and her description of her discomfort with Hughes' actions was clearly a form of opposition, according to the Court.

Justice Souter then turned to the policy justification for an expansive definition of "opposition." He explained that employers who wish to respond appropriately to complaints (or rumors) of sexual harassment need to "ferret out and put a stop to any discriminatory activity" in order to avoid liability under the nondiscrimination laws. Indeed, the Court ruled in 1998 in *Burlington Industries v. Ellerth* and *Faragher v. Boca Raton* (*SA 2d,* pp. 164–65) that an employer who responded promptly and effectively to complaints of discrimination could assert an "affirmative defense" to a subsequent claim of discrimination (unless some "tangible employment action" had been taken against the employee). Justice Souter explained that the approach of the lower courts in *Crawford* would undermine the rulings in *Ellerth* and *Faragher,* and would discourage employees from coming forward or from participating in an employer's internal investigation. If an employee could only claim retaliation after filing a formal complaint of discrimination, said Justice Souter, "prudent employees would have a good reason to keep quiet about Title VII offenses against themselves or against others." Noting that the fear of retaliation is the primary reason that employees do not complain about or report harassment, Justice Souter said that denying employees a remedy for retaliation would force them to file an external charge of harassment without going through the internal complaint process, which would limit the employee's ability to recover against an employer for harassment because, under *Faragher/Ellerth*, the employee "unreasonably failed to take advantage of . . . preventive or corrective opportunities provided by the employer." That, said Justice Souter, was an unacceptable "catch-22" situation that neither Title VII nor previous Court rulings supported.

Although Crawford had also stated a claim under the "participation" clause, the Court declined to reach that issue because she had satisfied the requirements of the "opposition" clause.

Burlington Industries and *Crawford*, taken together, demonstrate the significant legal problems that can occur if individuals who complain of harassment or discrimination, or who are asked to participate in investigations, can tie that activity to an adverse employment action such that they may claim retaliation. As a result of these rulings, it is likely to be more difficult for a defendant college to obtain summary judgment on a disciplined or dismissed employee's claim of retaliation.

****

A federal trial court ruling highlights the importance of careful drafting of a college or university's sexual harassment policy. Some institutions have adopted the definition of sexual harassment contained in the EEOC's guidelines that define sexual harassment under Title VII (*SA 2d*, p. 163). Despite the adoption of this language, some institutional policies, or interpretations of these policies, go well beyond the language of the Title VII sexual harassment guidelines and the interpretation by federal courts of sexual harassment jurisprudence. For example, a "zero tolerance" sexual harassment policy would not necessarily comply with the Title VII jurisprudence that harassment must be "severe or pervasive." The interpretation of this Title VII sexual harassment guidelines language was at issue in *Soloski v. Adams*, 600 F. Supp. 2d 1276 (N.D. Ga. 2009). Soloski, the dean of the journalism school at the University of Georgia, was accused of making two remarks to a subordinate that she characterized as sexual harassment. The university investigated and determined that Soloski had violated the university's sexual harassment policy, which adopted the Title VII definition of sexual harassment and explicitly referred to Title VII. Soloski was forced to resign his deanship and was instructed to undergo harassment training.

Soloski sued the university, claiming breach of contract, violations of his constitutional right to due process, and sex discrimination, among other claims.

The court ruled that the university officials had abused their discretion in finding that Soloski had violated the policy because his conduct did not meet the Title VII standard of "severe or pervasive." The court ordered the university to rescind its finding that Soloski had violated the policy. The court explained that it was acceptable for an institution to have a policy against sexual harassment that was broader than that contained in the Title VII guidelines, but because the policy in question specifically referenced that law and adopted the language of its guidelines, the university was required to apply that language and not to use an expansive definition that the policy did not contain.

****

The ruling of a federal appellate court provides some comfort to college administrators who must make credibility determinations in investigating complaints of sexual harassment and in deciding whether or not to discipline the alleged harasser. In *McCullough v. University of Arkansas for Medical Sciences*, 559 F.3d 855 (8th Cir. 2009), two women filed sexual harassment complaints against McCullough, the Computer Project Program Director. When McCullough was informed of the complaints, he filed sexual harassment complaints against the two women who had accused him. An investigation was conducted, and the investigators concluded that the two women were credible and that McCullough was not. Furthermore, neutral employees confirmed the women's version of the facts and not McCullough's. The dean dismissed McCullough for violating the harassment policy and for untruthfulness. McCullough then filed a sex discrimination claim and a first amendment claim of retaliation under Section 1983.

The trial court awarded summary judgment to the university, and McCullough appealed. The appellate court stated that "the critical inquiry in discrimination cases like this one is not whether the employee actually engaged in the conduct for which he was terminated, but whether the employer in good faith believed that the employee was guilty of the conduct justifying discharge" (559 F.3d at 861–62). The court found ample evidence in the record to support the dismissal decision, and no evidence that it was motivated by sex discrimination. The court also rejected McCullough's claim of retaliation for free speech, stating that McCullough's communications concerning the harassment allegations were not matters of public interest, but in his own self-interest.

4.5.2.2. Equal Pay Act. Replacing a staff member with one who is paid substantially more for performing the same job could expose the institution to liability under the Equal Pay Act. In *Dixon v. University of Toledo*, 638 F. Supp. 2d 847 (N.D. Ohio 2009), a federal trial court concluded that a salary difference of more than $40,000 paid to the male replacement for a female associate vice president could provide sufficient evidence of a sex-based motive for the salary difference such that the female plaintiff could establish a prima facie case of sex discrimination. Although the U.S. Supreme Court has not ruled on whether a plaintiff may use her successor's salary as evidence that she was underpaid on the basis of her sex, federal appellate courts in several circuits have ruled that she may. *Lawrence v. CNF Transp., Inc.,* 340 F.3d 486 (8th Cir. 2003); *Brinkley v. Harbour Rec. Club,* 180 F.3d 598 (4th Cir. 1999); *Arrington v. Cobb County,* 139 F.3d 865(11th Cir. 1998); *Dey v. Colt Constr. & Dev. Co.,* 28 F.3d 1446 (7th Cir. 1994); *EEOC v. First Citizens Bank,* 758 F.2d 397 (9th Cir. 1985); *Plemer v. Parsons-Gilbane,* 713 F.2d 1127 (5th Cir. 1983); *Dubowsky v. Stern, Lavinthal, Norgaard & Daly,* 922 F.Supp. 985 (D.N.J. 1996).

4.5.2.5. Americans with Disabilities Act and Rehabilitation Act of 1973. The Americans with Disabilities Act has been amended by the ADA Amendments Act, which took effect on January 1, 2009. The amendments retain the original definition of a "disability," but include language instructing courts to construe the definition of disability broadly. The amendments state that courts must not consider the effect of "mitigating measures" (such as medication or prosthetic devices) in determining whether an individual's impairment meets the law's definition of "disability." The amendments also include an illustrative list of "major life activities": caring for oneself, performing manual tasks, seeing, hearing, eating, sleeping, walking, standing, lifting, bending, speaking, breathing, learning, reading, concentrating, thinking, communicating, and working. Working had on occasion been rejected by courts as a major life activity.

The amendments also broaden the definition of "major life activity" to include "major bodily functions" such as functions of the immune system, normal cell growth, digestive, bowel, bladder, neurological, brain, respiratory, circulatory, endocrine, and reproductive functions. And the amendments note that an employee need not prove that he or she has a disability in order to state a claim that the employer regarded the employee as disabled.

Given the broadening of the definition of disability, it is likely that courts will focus less on that issue and more directly on whether the individual was qualified for the position, with or without reasonable accommodation, and whether the accommodation the employee sought or was offered met the law's definition of "reasonable."

* * * *

Although the amendments to the Americans with Disabilities Act, passed in 2008, are expected to make it less likely that a court will award summary judgment, a recent case demonstrates that courts are still scrutinizing a plaintiff's claims to be protected under the ADA, particularly with respect to the requirement that the employee be "qualified" and able to perform the "essential functions" of the position. In *Shin v. University of Maryland Medical System Corporation,* 369 Fed. Appx. 472 (4th Cir. 2010), a federal appellate court affirmed a summary judgment ruling for the employer of an intern with serious performance problems. According to the hospital, the plaintiff prescribed incorrect medicine dosages, misdiagnosed patients, and required substantial assistance from supervisors and colleagues in order to complete his work. He was given a performance improvement plan and fewer patients to care for, but his performance did not improve. When Shin's performance did not improve, he requested a series of accommodations, such as fewer patients, additional time to record information, and a "more compassionate environment." These accommodations were denied because he would not have been able to meet the requirements for patient load of the Accreditation Council for Graduate Medical Education. The hospital sent him for a medical evaluation, which revealed attention deficit disorder, and he was prescribed medication and given a leave of absence. His condition did not improve with medication and rehabilitation. He was dismissed, and he sued, claiming that the hospital had failed to accommodate him.

The trial court ruled that Shin might be able to show that the hospital regarded him as disabled, but that he could not demonstrate that he was qualified because he could not perform the essential functions of an intern, with or without accommodation. His performance problems required substantial extra time of his supervisors and compromised patient care and safety, said the court. The appellate court affirmed the trial court's award of summary judgment to the hospital.

* * * *

Employees who do not notify their employers of the existence of an impairment or their need for accommodation cannot state claims under the Americans with Disabilities Act, according to a federal appellate court. In *Kobus v. College of St. Scholastica Inc.*, 608 F.3d 1034 (8th Cir. 2010), a painter employed by the college was diagnosed with depression, but did not advise the college either of the impairment or his need for accommodation. Although he was offered a leave when he spoke informally with a supervisor about a "mental health leave," he did not provide documentation of the need for the leave, and was terminated for excessive absences. The court affirmed the trial court's award of summary judgment to the college, and rejected EEOC Guidance advice that if an employee indicates that he or she is "depressed and stressed," the employer is alerted that the employee is requesting reasonable accommodation (Question 17, EEOC Notice No. 915.002, Enforcement Guidance on the Americans with Disabilities Act and Psychiatric Disabilities (Mar. 25, 1997), available at http://www.ipacweb.org/files/eeoc-psych.pdf). The court noted that EEOC regulations (29 C.F.R. §1630.9) indicate that an employee seeking an accommodation must notify the employer that an accommodation is needed.

4.5.2.6. Age Discrimination in Employment Act. For over a decade it has been unclear whether plaintiffs may use the "disparate impact" theory (see *SA 2d*, Sec. 5.2.1) to attack alleged discrimination that is unintentional under the Age Discrimination in Employment Act (ADEA), although this theory is available to plaintiffs under Title VII of the Civil Rights Act of 1964. The U.S. Supreme Court has resolved that issue in plaintiffs' favor, but in a way that is narrower than the theory's interpretation under Title VII.

In *Smith v. City of Jackson*, 544 U.S. 228 (2005), the court addressed the claim of a group of police officers who asserted that the city's method of allocating salary increases had a disproportionately negative impact on officers over the age of forty. In order to recruit and retain beginning officers by raising starting salaries to the level of starting police salaries in surrounding communities, the city had given proportionately higher salary increases to officers with seniority of five years or less. Although a few individuals who were older than forty were in this group, most of the over-forty officers had more than five years of seniority and received a proportionately smaller raise.

The Court ruled 8–0 that the disparate impact theory may be used in ADEA claims. It explained that federal judges had routinely allowed plaintiffs to state disparate impact claims under the ADEA until the Court's 1993 decision in *Hazen Paper Co. v. Biggins*, 507 U.S. 604 (1993), in which the Court had stated that it specifically was not addressing whether a disparate impact claim could be brought under the ADEA. The Court addressed the language in the ADEA that permits an employer to take an action that would otherwise violate that law if a "reasonable factor other than age" (RFOA) is the justification, even if that "reasonable factor" is linked to the employee's age. In *Hazen Paper,* the employer had discharged a worker just before his pension would have vested. The Court had ruled that it was the anticipated vesting, not the plaintiff's age, that was the reason for the discharge, and that the employer had not violated the ADEA because the employer's reason was a "reasonable factor other than age."

The court stated that the RFOA language in the ADEA means that the scope of disparate impact liability under the ADEA is narrower than under Title VII. In a disparate impact case brought under Title VII, the defendant employer must demonstrate that the challenged "neutral practice" is a "business necessity." Under the ADEA, the "neutral practice" need only be "reasonable" and not facially related to the employee's age. The Court then ruled that the city's decision to base salary increases on rank and seniority was a RFOA and thus did not violate the ADEA.

> While there may have been other reasonable ways for the City to achieve its goals, the one selected was not unreasonable. Unlike the business necessity test, which asks whether there are other ways for the employer to achieve its goals that do not result in a disparate impact on a protected class, the reasonableness inquiry includes no such requirement. [544 U.S. at 243.]

Although the ruling in *City of Jackson* may initially stimulate more disparate impact claims brought by older workers, the lighter burden borne by the employer to demonstrate that its actions were "reasonable" rather than discriminatory will make these claims more difficult to win than disparate impact claims brought under Title VII.

∗ ∗ ∗ ∗

The U.S. Supreme Court has clarified the plaintiff's burden of production in making a prima facie case of age discrimination. In *Gross v. FBL Financial Services*, 129 S. Ct. 2343 (2009), the plaintiff filed an age discrimination claim after he was demoted. He attempted to use the mixed-motive analysis approved by the Supreme Court in *Price Waterhouse v. Hopkins*, 490 U.S. 228 (1989), a case brought under Title VII, claiming that age was one of several motives for his demotion. The Supreme Court, in a 5–4 decision, rejected his use of the mixed-motive theory under the ADEA, saying that a plaintiff must show that age was the "but-for" cause of the challenged adverse employment action, and that the Court has never authorized the burden-shifting or mixed-motive models used by Title VII for lawsuits brought under the ADEA.

4.5.2.7. Genetic Information Nondiscrimination Act (new subsection). The Genetic Information Nondiscrimination Act (GINA), Pub. L. 110–233, 122 Stat. 881, codified at 42 U.S.C. 2000ff et seq., was signed into law on May 21, 2008. Title I of the law regulates how insurance companies use genetic information in making coverage decisions. Title II applies to employers and is enforced by the EEOC.

GINA is modeled after Title VII in that it applies to all employers with 15 or more employees and requires an individual to file an EEOC charge alleging a GINA violation before filing a lawsuit in federal court. The law prohibits covered employers from using genetic information about an applicant or employee to make employment decisions, restricts the deliberate (as opposed to involuntary) collection of genetic information, and limits the disclosure of such information by employers.

The EEOC has issued final regulations for Title II of GINA. 75 *Fed. Reg.* 68912–68939 (November 9, 2010). The regulations define "genetic information" as information from genetic tests, the genetic tests of family members, family medical history, and genetic information of a fetus carried by an individual or an individual's family member or an embryo lawfully held by an individual or family member receiving assistive reproductive services. Genetic information also includes information about an individual's or family member's request for or receipt of genetic services or participation in clinical research that includes genetic services. Prohibited employment actions under GINA are the same as those prohibited by Title VII, and retaliation against an individual who opposes any act made unlawful by GINA, files a charge of discrimination under GINA or assists another in doing so, or testifies in connection with such a charge is also prohibited.

The regulations also specify that any genetic information about an employee or family member must be treated as a confidential medical record and protected from disclosure.

4.5.2.8. Constitutional prohibitions against employment discrimination. A federal appellate court has clarified the circumstances under which a plaintiff alleging age discrimination by a state college or university can state a claim in federal court. In *Ahlmeyer v. Nevada System of Higher Education*, 555 F.3d 1051 (9th Cir. 2009), a staff member at a Nevada public college claimed that her supervisor treated her more harshly than her younger coworkers. Because the *Kimel* (*SA 2d*, pp. 175–76) doctrine prevented her from suing the public university system under the ADEA, she attempted to sue her supervisor personally under Section 1983, alleging violations of the Fourteenth Amendment equal protection clause. The court dismissed her constitutional claim, stating that the ADEA was the exclusive enforcement mechanism for workplace age discrimination, and thus she could not attack alleged age discrimination using an equal protection theory.

4.5.2.11. Transgender (new subsection). A federal trial court ruled that discrimination against a transgendered individual is a form of sex discrimination and violates Title VII. In *Schroer v. Billington*, 577 F. Supp. 2d 293 (D.D.C. 2008), the plaintiff had applied for a position at the Library of Congress. The plaintiff, who presented as a male during the job interview, was offered a position as a terrorism-related policy analyst. When the plaintiff informed his prospective supervisor that he would be transitioning to a female gender, the job offer was rescinded. The plaintiff had an extensive military career and was considered to be well qualified for the position, but the supervisor stated that she did not believe that the plaintiff could function in the position as a transgendered individual. The court ruled that all of the defendant's reasons for rescinding the job offer were pretextual and were based upon stereotypes about transgendered individuals, which violated Title VII's prohibition against discrimination on the basis of sex. For a discussion of the legal issues related to discrimination on the basis of transgendered status, see Ann C. McGinley. "Erasing Boundaries: Masculinities, Sexual Minorities, and Employment Discrimination." 43 *Michigan Journal of Law Reform* 713 (2010). And for an essay on one of the flashpoints in the conflict over the rights of transgendered individuals at work—restroom use—see Jill D. Weinberg. "Transgender Bathroom Usage: A Privileging of Biology and Physical Difference in the Law." 18 *Buff. Women's L. J.* 147 (2010).

As of November 2010, twelve states and the District of Columbia, and 109 cities and counties prohibited employers from discriminating against individuals on the basis of gender identity or expression, and another two states prohibited public employers from such discrimination. Pennsylvania prohibits such discrimination in state government. States that prohibit employment discrimination in both the public and private sectors are California, Colorado, District of Columbia, Iowa, Illinois, Maine, Minnesota, New Jersey, New Mexico, Oregon, Rhode Island, Vermont, and Washington (www.transgenderlaw.org).

Sec. 4.7. *Application of Nondiscrimination Laws to Religious Institutions*

A U.S. Court of Appeals has directly addressed the issue of whether the First Amendment's religion clauses (or Title VII itself) may protect a religious educational institution that engages in sex or race discrimination prohibited by Title VII when such discrimination is based on religious belief (see *SA 2d*, p. 195). In *Curay-Cramer v. Ursaline Academy*, 450 F.3d 130 (3d Cir. 2006), a dismissed female instructor argued that her dismissal constituted sex discrimination because the defendant Academy had treated her more harshly than the male employees who had committed similar offenses. The court determined that an analysis of the plaintiff's claim would implicate the Academy's religious mission and its religious reasons for the dismissal. "We [the court] would have to measure the degree of severity of various violations of church doctrine." "[W]e would be meddling in matters related to a religious organization's ability to define the parameters of what constitutes orthodoxy." It would be "impossible to avoid inquiry into a religious employer's religious mission or the plausibility of its religious justification for an employment decision."

The court thus concluded that, when a religious employer's religious mission would be jeopardized in this way by a court's review of a gender (or race) discrimination claim, the court may not proceed. Court review under such circumstances would raise "serious constitutional questions" under the religion clauses. Moreover, in the legislative history of Title VII, "Congress has not manifested an affirmative intention to apply the statute to a religious employer in the face of such constitutional difficulties."

In effect, the court in *Ursaline Academy* has created an exception to the general understanding that Title VII's prohibition of gender and race discrimination applies to religious institutions (see *SA 2d*, pp. 192–94). The court makes clear that this is a limited exception and that many gender (and presumably race) discrimination claims would not raise serious constitutional issues under the religion clauses.

Sec. 4.8. Faculty Academic Freedom and Freedom of Expression

4.8.1. General concepts and principles

4.8.1.1. Faculty freedom of expression in general. Soderstrand v. Oklahoma, ex rel. Board of Regents of Oklahoma Agricultural and Mechanical Colleges, 463 F. Supp.2d 1308 (2006), illustrates the application of *O'Connor v. Ortega*, and the Fourth Amendment generally, to college and university officials' search and seizure of office computers while investigating allegedly work-related misconduct (see *SA 2d*, pp. 209–10). A university employee had found pictures and images on CDs that appeared to be child pornography in a lock box kept in a storage room that was part of a faculty office complex. After attributing ownership of the box to Dr. Soderstrand, who was a university department head, two members of the OSU computing security office entered Dr. Soderstrand's office and seized the hard drive from his desktop computer as well as his *personal* laptop computer. The laptop computer screen displayed the university-supported e-mail client and showed various spreadsheets that appeared to contain office records. The desktop hard drive and personal laptop computer were taken without a warrant and without the consent of Dr. Soderstrand, who was not in the office. University police retained the laptop after reviewing its contents.

Dr. Soderstrand eventually filed a Section 1983 action claiming that university personnel had unreasonably searched and seized his laptop in violation of the Fourth Amendment. In analyzing the claim, the court outlined the factors to be considered in determining the constitutionality of a public employer's warrantless search effectuated while investigating an employee's alleged work-related misconduct: "whether the action was justified at its inception and whether the search as actually conducted was reasonably related in scope to the circumstances, which justified the interference in the first place."

The court determined that the seizure of the laptop was "reasonable" under *O'Connor*:

> Here, as in *O'Connor*, the office being searched was the office of a professional working for a public institution, and the search was to investigate work-related misconduct. In this case, the suspected misconduct involved possible child pornography stored on computers located in Dr. Soderstrand's office on campus. It is undisputed that OSU security officers entered plaintiff's OSU office and seized the hard drive of the desk top computer and plaintiff's laptop computer, and that the laptop computer was open, on and running at the time, with an OSU supported email program on the screen and with various spreadsheets that appeared to contain office records.
>
> Applying the standards of *O'Connor*, and construing all facts and allegations in plaintiff's favor, the court finds and concludes that the search was justified at its inception and that its scope was reasonably related to the circumstances which justified it. [463 F. Supp.2d at 1314.]

The search and seizure therefore did not violate the Fourth Amendment rights of Dr. Soderstrand, and the defendants were entitled to summary judgment.

Prior to this civil case, the federal government had instituted a criminal case against Dr. Soderstrand based on child pornography charges; see *United States v. Soderstrand*, 412 F.3d 1146 (10th Cir. 2005). The court's opinion in the criminal case provides additional facts and analysis of the Fourth Amendment issues that usefully supplement the federal district court's analysis in the later civil case (above), in particular with respect to the validity of the university employee's original search of the lock box in the supply room.

4.8.1.6. "Institutional" academic freedom. One strand of the ongoing debate about "institutional" academic freedom is focused on the First Amendment status of public colleges and universities. Some of the recent scholarship that supports this strand is challenging the classical position that governmental entities do not have any constitutional rights of their own under the Bill of Rights—regardless of whether First Amendment rights are at issue or rights under some other amendment, and regardless of whether or not the government entity is a public college or university. The classical position is based on the theoretical underpinnings of the Constitution, the Bill of Rights, and the Fourteenth Amendment, as revealed in the writings on American constitutionalism, the adoption debates, and various opinions of the U.S. Supreme Court; as well as on the implications of the text of the various rights clauses, which generally grant rights to "person(s)" or the "people," as distinguished from government.

One leading article argues that the purposes of the First Amendment speech and press clauses suggest that "state actors" may sometimes have speech and press rights, and that "government speech" may thus sometimes be protected by the First Amendment (David Fagundes, "State Actors as First Amendment Speakers," 100 *Northwestern U.L. Rev.* 1637 (2006); *contra*, Randall Bezanson & William Buss, "The Many Faces of Government Speech, 86 *Iowa L. Rev.* 1377 (2001)). Another article argues that public universities, in particular, have First Amendment rights in some circumstances that they may assert, like private universities, against other state actors (and against the federal government) in order to protect their academic missions and unique role in advancing public discourse (Paul Horwitz, "Universities as First Amendment Institutions: Some Easy Answers and Hard Questions," 54 *UCLA L. Rev.* 1497 (2007)). If such arguments were accepted by the courts, they would obviously strengthen public colleges' and universities' claims that institutional academic freedom is a First Amendment right. But to date, those courts that have recognized institutional academic freedom have not embraced these arguments as such and, indeed, have not developed any conceptual basis for grounding public institutions' claims in the First Amendment. The U.S. Supreme Court's statements on academic freedom in *Grutter v. Bollinger*, 539 U.S. 306 (2003), relied upon by both articles cited above and by some courts as well, do not themselves provide strong support for the claim that public institutions have First Amendment rights (see *SA 2d*, p. 214). The same may be said of the Court's earlier statements in *Regents of University of Michigan v. Ewing* (see, *SA 2d*, p. 213). Nor has there been any clear indication by other courts that they are ready to set aside the classical view of constitutional rights (above) or the public-private dichotomy in higher education law (see *SA 2d*, Sec. 1.5) to the extent necessary to accommodate the claim that public colleges and universities have their own First Amendment rights to academic freedom. Recently, in *Coalition to Defend Affirmative Action v. Granholm*, 473 F. 3d 237 (6th Cir. 2006), a case involving several Michigan universities, one U.S. Court of Appeals specifically declined to travel this pathway, emphasizing that

> The Universities mistake *interests* grounded in the First Amendment—including their interests in selecting student bodies—with First Amendment *rights*. It is not clear, for example, how the Universities, as subordinate organs of the State, have First Amendment rights against the State or its voters. *See, e.g., Trustees of Dartmouth Coll. v. Woodward*, 4 Wheat. 518, 17 U.S. 629 (1819). One does not generally think of the First Amendment as protecting the State from the people but the other way around—of the Amendment protecting individuals from the state. [473 F.3d at 247.]

* * * *

In a subsequent case, *Pleasant Grove City v. Summum*, 129 S. Ct. 1125 (2009), the U.S. Supreme Court explicitly supported the classical view that only private speakers have First Amendment rights. In a complex case involving a city but apparently applicable as well to public universities, the Court determined that the challenged activity of the city "is best viewed as a form of government speech" and therefore "is not subject to the free Speech Clause."

In so holding, the Court analyzed at length the distinction between "government speech" and "private speech," emphasizing that

> [If the city officials] were engaging in their own expressive conduct, then the Free Speech Clause has no application. The Free Speech Clause restricts government regulation of private speech; it does not regulate government speech. See *Columbia Broadcasting System, Inc. v. Democratic National Committee,* 412 U.S. 94, 139, n.7 (1973) (Stewart, J., concurring). [129 S. Ct. at 1131.]

On the other hand, the Court also reaffirmed that

> A government entity has the right to "speak for itself." *Board of Regents of Univ. of Wis. System v. Southworth,* 529 U.S. 217, 229 (2000). "[I]t is entitled to say what it wishes," *Rosenberger v. Rector and Visitors of Univ. of Va.,* 515 U.S. 819, 833 (1995), and to select the views that it wants to express. See *Rust v. Sullivan,* 500 U.S. 173, 194 (1991). [129 S. Ct. at 1131.]

When a government entity speaks "for itself" by "delivering a government-controlled message," the speech is not subject to the restrictions of the free speech clause (for example, the requirement of viewpoint neutrality). This "government speech" concept provides strong support for the institutional autonomy interests of colleges and universities (see *SA 2d,* p. 214).

4.8.2. Academic freedom in teaching

4.8.2.1. In general. The U.S. Supreme Court's 2006 decision in *Garcetti v. Ceballos* (*SA 2d,* p. 199) potentially has many substantial effects on court precedents and future cases on faculty academic freedom in public institutions. The case of *Renken v. Gregory,* 541 F.3d 769 (7th Cir. 2008), illustrates the restrictive effects that *Garcetti* could have on faculty speech relating to teaching, even beyond the classroom.

In *Renken,* a tenured professor at the University of Wisconsin-Milwaukee had applied for a federal grant that NSF awarded to the university, subject to its providing matching funds. The dean of the university's engineering school sent the professors involved a proposal about the conditions attached to the university's matching funds. Renken took issue with the proposal, believing that it contravened NSF regulations. He wrote a letter to the dean "cataloguing a list of criticisms regarding the project" and filed a complaint against the dean with the chair of the university committee. Renken thereafter exchanged letters with the dean and wrote other university officials, continuing his complaints about the university's handling of the grant. After Renken rejected a final compromise proposal prepared by the dean of the graduate school, the university decided to return the grant money to NSF.

Renken asserted that his criticisms were protected speech under the First Amendment and that the university had retaliated against him because of those criticisms. When he filed suit, the district court granted the university's motion for summary judgment because, under *Garcetti,* Renken had spoken as an employee and not as a private citizen. The appellate court affirmed.

In its opinion, the court gave no attention to a possible scholarship and teaching exception to *Garcetti*, focusing only on whether Renken had spoken as an employee.

Renken argued "that the tasks that he conducted in relation to the grant were implemented at his discretion '*while* in the course of his job and not as a *requirement* of his job'"; that "his job duties did not extend to making formal complaints"; and that "it was '[s]olely by the terms of the Grant, *not* his job,' [that he] was required to complain" of fiscal improprieties. The appellate court responded that these distinctions were not relevant to the *Garcetti* concept of employee speech. Either way, Renken was acting within his scope of his employment:

> In fulfillment of his acknowledged teaching and service responsibilities, Renken acted as a PI [principal investigator], applying for the NSF grant. This grant aided in the fulfillment of his teaching responsibilities because, as Renken notes in his reply brief, the grant was an education grant for the benefit of students as "undergraduate education development. . . ." In his capacity as PI, Renken . . . . complained to several levels of University officials about the various difficulties he encountered in the course of administering the grant as a PI. Thereby, Renken called attention to fund misuse relating to a project that he was in charge of administering as a University faculty member. In so doing, Renken was speaking as a faculty employee, and not as a private citizen, because administering the grant as a PI fell within the teaching and service duties that he was employed to perform . . . . Here, by Renken's own admission, his employment status as full professor depended on the administration of grants, such as the NSF grant. It was in the course of that administration, that Renken made his statements about funding improprieties within the confines of the University system and as the principal PI. [541 F. 3d at 773–74.]

The court consistently categorized the professor's work on the grant as part of his "teaching duties." With other types of grants and in other contexts, however, similar issues could arise under a faculty member's research duties or governance duties. In all these arenas, the *Renken* case appears to be decidedly unfavorable to whistleblowers and to the concept of whistle-blowing as a constraint on governmental abuse of power. In the foundational *Connick* case itself (*SA 2d*, Sec. 4.8.1), the Court spoke of the importance of employees' "inform[ing] the public that [a government office] was not discharging its governmental responsibilities . . . [and] bring[ing] to light actual or potential wrongdoing or breach of public trust on the part of [government officials]" (461 U.S. 138, 148 (1983)). This objective is undermined by the *Garcetti* employee speech doctrine as applied in cases such as *Renken*, thus enhancing the need for effective statutory protection for employee whistleblowers.

4.8.2.2. The classroom. The applicability of the U.S. Supreme Court's decision in *Garcetti v. Ceballos* (see *SA 2d*, p. 199) to classroom speech is still unresolved. One federal appellate court has recently evinced some sympathy for the argument that *Garcetti*'s rejection of First Amendment protection for "employee speech" should not apply to "expression related to academic scholarship or classroom instruction" (*Gorum v. Sessoms*, 561 F. 3d 179, 186 (3d Cir. 2009), quoting *Garcetti,* 547 U.S. at 425, 438, opinions of Kennedy, J., & Souter, J.). But this court also noted that, should an exception from *Garcetti* be developed for higher education faculty members, that would then lead to various issues regarding when professional "employee" speech is "related to academic scholarship or classroom instruction" and thus eligible for the exception.

One court has recognized an exception from *Garcetti* for faculty classroom speech. In a medical school case, *Kerr v. Hurd,* 694 F. Supp. 2d 817 (S.D. Ohio 2010), the district court determined that the issue of a scholarship and teaching exception was left unresolved in *Garcetti,* and that the district court would therefore follow precedent in its own district and circuit, which supported a classroom speech exception from *Garcetti's* employee speech doctrine. The court then made this statement:

> Even without the binding precedent, this Court would find an academic exception to *Garcetti.* Recognizing an academic freedom exception to *Garcetti* analysis is important to protecting First Amendment values. Universities should be the active trading floors in the marketplace of ideas. Public universities should be no different from private universities in that respect. At least where, as here, the expressed views are well within the range of accepted medical opinion, they should certainly receive First Amendment protection, particularly at the university level. See Justice Souter's dissent in *Garcetti,* citing *Keyishian v. Bd. of Regents,* 385 U.S. 589 (1967). [694 F. Supp. 2d at 843–44.]

Selected Annotated Bibliography

Sec. 4.5. (Employment Discrimination)

Weitzner, Richard A. *Religious Discrimination and Accommodation Issues in Higher Education: A Legal Compendium.* (Nat'l Ass'n. of College & Univ. Attys., 2006). Discusses religious discrimination and accommodation in employment and the religious exercise rights of students; constitutional issues and the public employer; the religiously affiliated institution; religious harassment; religion and academic freedom, religion versus cultural accommodation, proselytizing in the workplace, and prayer in the academy. Includes sample policies and forms and federal regulations and guidance.

Sec. 4.8. (Faculty Academic Freedom and Freedom of Expression)

Gerstmann, Evan, & Streb, Matthew (eds.). *Academic Freedom at the Dawn of a New Century: How Terrorism, Governments, and Culture Wars Impact Free Speech* (Stanford Univ. Press, 2006). A timely and highly pertinent exploration of cutting-edge issues and perspectives on academic freedom. Contains ten essays by ten experts. Contributions include "Academic Freedom in the Post September 11 Era: An Old Game with New Rules," by Robert O'Neil, and three essays that develop a fruitful "global perspective" on academic freedom in various other countries compared with the United States.

Olswang, Steven, & Cameron, Cheryl (eds.). *Academic Freedom and Tenure: A Legal Compendium* (Nat'l Ass'n of College & Univ. Attys., 2006) (2 vols.). Includes materials on the history and purpose of academic freedom and tenure; who academic freedom protects; collective bargaining; what tenure and academic freedom don't protect; tenure as a mechanism to protect a faculty members' academic freedom; procedural protections of tenure; the tenure contract; and alternatives to tenure.

O'Neil, Robert. *Academic Freedom in the Wired World: Political Extremism, Corporate Power and the University* (Harvard Univ. Press, 2008). A probing overview and analysis of academic freedom's modern evolution, and emerging threats to academic freedom, in the early twenty-first century and beyond. Problems addressed include cyberspace communications, especially blogs and Web sites; threats to academic freedom coming from the private sector; and academic freedom in times of crisis. Focuses on the tension between institutional interests and individual interests regarding academic freedom, the very limited protection that courts now provide for faculty academic freedom, and the need for academics to work together on new ways of conceptualizing and protecting academic freedom.

White, Lawrence. "Fifty Years of Academic Freedom Jurisprudence." 36 *J. Coll. & Univ. Law* 791 (2010). Traces over fifty years of academic freedom jurisprudence; argues that courts have been unwilling or unable to provide a "unitary, coherent, or (above all) useful meaning" to the term.

5

The Legal Status of Students

Sec. 5.2. *The Contractual Rights of Students*

A Florida appellate court has provided a thoughtful analysis in rejecting a student's attempt to argue that a university cannot change the terms of its student handbook, or its graduation requirements, while the student is enrolled. In *Jallali v. Nova Southeastern University*, 992 So.2d 338 (Fla. Dist. Ct. App. 2008), the appellate court overturned a jury award of $819,000 on the student's breach of contract claim, ruling that the trial court should have directed a verdict for the university. Jallali, a student of osteopathic medicine, had entered the medical school in 1998 and expected to graduate in 2002, but failed so many subjects during his first year that he had to retake them, which pushed his expected graduation year to 2003. During his second year, the university changed the requirements for graduation, stating that students who graduated in 2003 or later must pass two national examinations. The previous graduation requirement stated that students could take the second exam up to six years after completing their other requirements. Jallali was unable to pass the second exam, even after the medical school allowed him a second chance to take it.

The appellate court rejected Jallali's argument that the medical school had breached its contract with him by changing the graduation requirements after he enrolled. First, noted the court, the student handbook specifically reserved the right to change curricular or other requirements "at any time." The court said that Jallali would have to prove that the changes were made arbitrarily and in bad faith, which he had not done. In fact, the graduation requirements had been changed in order to conform with new requirements of the agency that accredits colleges of osteopathic medicine. The court quoted both *Ewing* and *Horowitz* (*SA 2d,* p. 76), noting that judgments about a student's academic performance and qualifications to be a medical doctor should be made by the experts, not by the courts.

* * * *

Students challenging a college's decision to change from a single-sex institution to one that admits both sexes have tried, and failed, to state a breach of contract claim. Over the dissent of two justices, who believed that the case required a full hearing, the Supreme Court of Virginia rejected the attempt of current students to argue that a college's recruiting materials and other documents created a contract that promised to keep the college a women's college until they graduated. In *Dodge v. Trustees of Randolph-Macon College*, 661 S.E. 2d 801 (Va., 2008), the plaintiffs, nine current students at Randolph-Macon, contended that they had a contract with the college to receive an education in a "predominantly female environment" for four years, and asked the court to enjoin the transformation to a coeducational school until 2010 when they would have graduated. Although the plaintiffs produced acceptance letters, the college's catalog, and other correspondence concerning the single-sex nature of the college, the Virginia Supreme Court rejected their contention that these documents created a contract between the students and the college to maintain the college as a women's college until they graduated. Said the court: "There is no language in any of these documents in which the College made a clear, definite, and specific promise to operate a college predominantly for women during the duration of the plaintiffs' academic studies at the College." The court sustained the appellate court's dismissal of the complaint.

* * * *

The concept of fiduciary duty, once applied primarily in the higher education context to members of an institution's board of trustees and senior administrators, is now being discussed as a potential duty assumed by academic advisors, particularly with respect to the relationship between a graduate student and his or her thesis advisor. *Black's Law Dictionary* defines "fiduciary" as a relationship "founded on trust or confidence reposed by one person in the integrity and fidelity of another." It does not arise from contract, and typically requires a higher standard of conduct than the contractual concept of "good faith and fair dealing." Students have attempted to use this theory to argue that a graduate student is dependent upon the thesis advisor for assistance and support, and that the advisor must behave with complete integrity in carrying out his or her duties and always act in the best interest of the student.

In *Johnson v. Schmitz*, a case involving a dispute between a graduate student and his advisor, discussed in *SA 2d* on p. 249, the trial court also ruled that the student could proceed with his claim that the university had breached its fiduciary duty toward the student by not protecting him from alleged academic misconduct by his faculty advisors. Another state appellate court has rejected that theory, however. In *Swenson v. Bender*, 764 N.W.2d 596 (Minn.

Ct. App. 2009), a doctoral student who was enrolled at Cappella University, an all-online university, sued her former advisor for breach of a fiduciary duty. The student, Swenson, accused the advisor, Bender, an adjunct instructor at the university, of "stealing" her dissertation idea and falsely accusing the student of plagiarism. Although Bender was not the chair of Swenson's dissertation committee, she worked closely with Swenson and shared many of her ideas with her. The two had discussed collaborating on a coauthored book and article. At some point, disagreement arose about how to attribute credit for theoretical constructs the two had discussed while Bender was advising Swenson on her dissertation. Swenson accused Bender of "sabotaging" her efforts to obtain the doctoral degree and of "stealing" her ideas for use on Bender's academic Web site. Bender accused Swenson of plagiarism in her dissertation. The university's academic standards committee investigated, but took no position on the plagiarism accusations. They did conclude, however, that Bender acted unethically by developing a personal relationship with Swenson, but could not determine which material in Swenson's dissertation was her own and which should be attributed to Bender. The committee, which now no longer included Bender, required Swenson to rewrite her dissertation.

Swenson sued for conversion and breach of fiduciary duty. Although the trial court ruled for Swenson on the fiduciary duty claim, it rejected her conversion claim. Bender appealed. The appellate court reversed the trial court's ruling on the fiduciary duty claim. The trial court had based its ruling on three factors underpinning the relationship between a dissertation advisor and a doctoral student: (1) the relationship of trust and deference by the student; (2) the advisor's sole duty to assist the student with the dissertation; and (3) the student's reliance on the advisor in refining the dissertation and conducting the research and writing.

The appellate court stated that a dissertation committee member, even the chair, has an "independent obligation" to the university, and does not just act on behalf of the student. Furthermore, the court noted that a faculty member has an obligation to report plagiarism. Because Bender's obligations were in some respects contrary to Swenson's interests (her duty to be critical of the research and writing, her obligation to report academic misconduct), the court concluded that there could be no fiduciary duty between Swenson and Bender, and thus there was no breach.

In the context of a sexual harassment claim, however, a state's highest court approved of the use of fiduciary duty theory. In *Schneider v. Plymouth State College*, 744 A.2d 101 (N.H. 1999), the court ruled that the relationship between students and professors is built on trust, and that because students are subject to the power of the professor to award grades and provide reference letters, it is difficult for them to reject unwelcome sexual advances by a faculty member. Said the court,

> When the plaintiff enrolled at [the college], she became dependent on the
> defendants for her education, thereby requiring them 'to act in good faith
> and with due regard' for her interests . . . The relationship between students

and those that teach them is built on a professional relationship of trust and deference, rarely seen outside the academic community. As a result, we conclude that this relationship gives rise to a fiduciary duty on behalf of the defendants to create an environment in which the plaintiff could pursue her education free from sexual harassment by faculty members. [744 A.2d at 106, citations omitted.]

* * * *

A federal appellate court opinion, affirming an award of summary judgment to a private university that dismissed a student from a nurse anesthesia program on grounds of concern for patient safety, provides a good example of judicial deference to the academic judgments of faculty. In *Kimberg v. University of Scranton*, 2010 U.S. App. LEXIS 22565 (3d Cir. 10/27/10), the student argued that the university had breached its contract by placing him on probation and then dismissing him. The court rejected his arguments, ruling that the trial court had reviewed substantial evidence of the plaintiff's inadequate clinical performance, and that such an academic judgment was clearly supported by the evidence.

Sec. 5.3. *Student Academic Freedom*

In *Ward v. Wilbanks*, 2010 WL 3026428 (E.D. Mich. 2010), the court relied on *Brown v. Li* and *Axson-Flynn* (*SA 2d*, pp. 255–60) to reject the First Amendment free speech claims of a student who had been dismissed from a master's degree program in counseling at Eastern Michigan University. In granting summary judgment to the defendants, the court also relied on the U.S. Supreme Court's decision in *Hazelwood School District v. Kuhlmeier*, 484 U.S. 260 (1988), and the "legitimate pedagogical concerns" test established in that case—as had the courts in both *Brown* and *Axson-Flynn*.

The university officials in *Ward* had charged the student with "refus[ing] to accept a gay person as a client in practicum" for the reason "that counseling gay people about relationship issues violates your religious beliefs," and with being "unwilling to change this behavior" (letters to student from counseling program personnel). The officials claimed that the student's inability to "set aside [your] personal values or belief systems and work with the value system of the client" violated the American Counseling Association Code of Ethics. (The Student Handbook required all students in the counseling program to comply with this Code of Ethics.) After an informal, and then a formal, hearing on these charges, the student was dismissed from the program.

In court, the student claimed (as had the students in *Brown v. Li* and *Axson-Flynn*) that the dismissal violated her free speech rights. Rejecting her arguments, the court determined that the student's "refusal to counsel the client in question constitutes a refusal to complete a curriculum requirement," that this requirement and program's policy on counseling are "reasonably related to legitimate pedagogical concerns," and that the officials' reasons for dismissing the student were supported by the ACA Code of Ethics and were not "a mere pretext to retaliate against her for expressing her religious beliefs."

The student also claimed (as had the student in *Axson-Flynn*) that the dismissal violated her free exercise rights. Rejecting these arguments as well, and relying in part on the free exercise principles in *Axson-Flynn* (*SA 2d*, pp. 259–60), the court determined that

> [T]he Program's requirement that counseling students adhere to the ACA Code of Ethics . . applies equally to all students enrolled in the Program, and . . . it is a core component of the Practicum course. The Program's requirements apply to everyone equally, regardless of religion, and are "not aimed at particular religious practices." There is no system of "particularized exemptions" by which students enrolled in the Program would be allowed to deviate from the ACA Code of Ethics in order to refer all clients whose behavior or sexual orientation they found objectionable. [2010 WL at *17, quoting *Kissinger v. Board of Trustees of Ohio State University*, 5 F.3d 177, 179 (6th Cir. 1993).]

The court in *Ward* also relied on the earlier *Kissinger* case (above), in which the court rejected the free exercise claim of a veterinary student who had objected, on religious grounds, to a course requirement that she operate on healthy animals for training purposes.

Less than a month after the decision in *Ward v. Wilbanks*, another district court issued its decision in a similar case involving free speech and free exercise claims brought by another graduate student in a counseling program. In *Keeton v. Anderson-Wiley*, 733 F. Supp. 2d 1368 (S.D. Ga. 2010), the court denied the plaintiff's motion for a preliminary injunction. Citing and quoting *Ward*, the court used similar reasoning to support its decision. It would be prudent to be watching for an appellate court decision in one or both of these cases. (*Ward* and *Keeton* are also discussed in Section 8.2 of this *Supplement*.)

* * * *

Issues about required exercises and training programs for students (see *SA 2d*, p. 261) also arose in the *Keeton* case (immediately above in this *Supplement*). Program officials had required the plaintiff student to complete diversity "sensitivity training" focusing particularly on counseling clients who are gay, lesbian, bisexual, transgender, or queer/questioning. The student claimed that this requirement violated her free speech rights. The court denied the student's motion for a preliminary injunction.

Sec. 5.4. Students' Legal Relationships with Other Students

In an October 26, 2010 "guidance letter," the U.S. Department of Education has focused on the problem of "bullying" that has been escalating in both higher education and K–12 education in recent years. The Department acknowledges in the letter that it "focuses on the elementary and secondary school context" but that "the legal principles also apply to postsecondary institutions . . . ."

The letter frames bullying as conduct that may constitute "discriminatory harassment" by peers under federal civil rights laws enforced by the Department's Office for Civil Rights (OCR). Bullying a gay student, for example, may be covered by Title IX because "it can be sex discrimination if students are harassed either for exhibiting what is perceived as a stereotypical characteristic for their sex, or for failing to conform to stereotypical notions of masculinity and femininity"; and such coverage may apply "regardless of the actual or perceived sexual orientation or gender identity of the harasser or target." (See generally pp. 7–8 of letter on sexual orientation harassment.) The letter also explains and clarifies schools' and colleges' responsibilities to combat bullying under the laws enforced by OCR, and suggests various good practices and various resources for K–12 schools and higher educational institutions. The letter may be found at http://www2.ed.gov/about/offices/list/ocr/letters/colleague-201010.pdf.

The Office for Civil Rights issued another "Dear Colleague" letter on April 4, 2011 that addresses institutions' responsibilities under Title IX when students report that they have been sexually assaulted. The letter may be found at http://www2.ed.gov/about/offices/list/ocr/letters/colleague-201104.html.

****

Clarification. The case of *Simpson v. University of Colorado Boulder* (*SA 2d*, p. 268) was settled in December 2007. The settlement agreement, in which the university did not admit any liability, provided that the university would pay substantial sums of money to the women plaintiffs and would also appoint a new official to advise the university on sexual harassment prevention and add another counselor to its office of victim's assistance. For further information, go to http://www.insidehighered.com/layout/set/print/news/2007/12/06/settle.

Sec. 5.5. *Student Files and Records*

5.5.1. *Family Educational Rights and Privacy Act (FERPA).* New

regulations interpreting FERPA became effective on January 8, 2009. The new regulations clarify the circumstances under which institutions may notify parents, using information that otherwise would be protected by FERPA: (1) if the student is a dependent for federal income tax purposes (§99.31(a)(8)); (2) if the disclosure is in connection with a health or safety emergency under the conditions specified in §99.36 (i.e., if knowledge of the information is necessary to protect the health or safety of the student or other individuals (§99.31(a)(10)); and (3) if the student has violated any federal, state, or local law, or any rule or policy of the institution, governing the use or possession of alcohol or a controlled substance, as long as the institution has determined that the student has committed a disciplinary violation regarding that use or possession and the student is under twenty-one at the time of the disclosure (§99.31(a)(15)). Section 99.31(a)(1)(i)(B) of the new regulations expands the definition of "school official" to include contractors, consultants, volunteers, or other entities to whom an institution may outsource certain activities or services that involve the use of education records. Section 99.31(a)(2) clarifies that institutions may share a student's education record with another institution that the student is planning to transfer to or does transfer to, including health and disciplinary records. And finally, the new regulations prohibit institutions from requiring students to sign a nondisclosure or confidentiality agreement when the institution informs a student victim of an alleged act of violence or non-forcible sex offense of the outcome of a disciplinary proceeding (Section 99.33(c)). (U.S. Department of Education, FERPA Final Rule, Section by Section Analysis, December 2008, available at www.ed.gov/policy/gen/guid/fpco/pdf/ht12–17–08-att.pdf.) The new rules may be found at 73 Fed. Reg. 74806 (December 9, 2008).

* * * *

A state trial court discussed a college or university's responsibilities when it receives a subpoena for documents that may be protected by FERPA. In *In Re: Subpoena Issued to Smith*, 921 N.E.2d 731 (Ohio Com. Pl. 2009), the Dean of Students of Xavier University was issued a grand jury subpoena for the production of documents that related to a student at the university. The university determined that the subpoena appeared to be lawfully issued, and notified the student of the demand for documents. The student did not contest the subpoena, but the dean asked the court for a ruling as to whether the university was permitted to provide the documents without the student's consent.

The court was critical of the university's request, saying:

> In general, only two things are required of a college or university that receives a
> subpoena. First, it must assure itself as to the facial validity of the subpoena or
> order. Then it must make a reasonable attempt to give notice to the student in
> sufficient time to allow a student to seek a protective order. The type of notice
> required will depend on the circumstances of each case. . . . The school has
> no obligation under FERPA to oppose an order or seek to quash a subpoena.
> Notice to the student or parents gives them the opportunity to bring before
> the court any objection they have to the requested disclosure and production.
> This opportunity has been afforded here, and the student has not sought to bar
> production of any of the records by a motion to quash or modify the subpoena.
> [921 N.E.2d at 734, citations omitted.]

5.5.2. State law. There have been a number of rulings by federal and state courts as to whether a record that would otherwise be protected by FERPA loses that protection if identifying information about the student(s) is redacted. The courts have concluded that, if such redaction is done, FERPA does not apply because it no longer contains "information directly related to a student." See, for example, *United States v. Miami Univ.*, 294 F.3d 797 (6th Cir. 2002); *Ragusa v. Malverne Union Free Sch. Dist.*, 549 Supp. 2d 288 (E.D. N.Y. 2008); *Osborn v. Board of Regents of University of Wisconsin System*, 647

N.W.2d 158, 168 n. 11 (Wis. 2002); *Unincorporated Operating Div. of Indiana Newspapers, Inc. v. Trustees of Indiana Univ.*, 787 N.E.2d 893 (Ind. App. 2003); and *Bd. of Trs. v. Cut Bank Pioneer Press*, 160 P.3d 482 (Mont. 2007).

Selected Annotated Bibliography

Sec. 5.5. (Student Files and Records)

Tribbensee, Nancy. "Privacy and Confidentiality: Balance Student Rights and Campus Safety." 34 *J. Coll. & Univ. Law* 393 (2008). Discusses the requirements of FERPA and HIPAA related to the disclosure of information about students and the issues that arise respecting with whom and how to communicate such information. Provides examples of models used by colleges to balance concerns for student privacy with appropriate actions to enhance their safety.

6

Admissions and Financial Aid

Sec. 6.1. Admissions

6.1.1. Basic legal requirements. The University of California has a policy that requires admissions staff to review and approve high school courses involving religion or ethics taken by applicants in order to determine whether these courses may be counted toward the required number of high school courses presented by applicants for admission. In *Association of Christian Schools International v. Stearns*, 362 Fed. Appx. 640 (9th Cir. 2010), a federal appellate court rejected the claims of an association of Christian schools that the University of California's review policy violated the free speech, free expression, free exercise, and equal protection clauses of the U.S. Constitution. According to the court, the challenged policy "provides that in order to receive UC approval, religion and ethics courses should 'treat the study of religion or ethics from the standpoint of scholarly inquiry, rather than in a manner limited to one denomination or viewpoint.'"

The court rejected all of the plaintiffs' constitutional challenges to the policy, both facial and as applied. The admissions staff used consistent guidelines to evaluate the courses, said the court, and their review did not favor or disfavor any particular religion. Nor did the policy encourage viewpoint discrimination, because the staff had approved a variety of religion courses that included religious texts and religious doctrine. The issue, said the court, was whether the course treated religion in a scholarly fashion, or was limited to one denomination or viewpoint. The policy did not suppress speech, or punish schools for teaching these courses or students for taking them, said the court. The intent of the policy was to ensure that students were prepared for "the rigors of academic study at UC." Furthermore, said the court, the policy did not violate the Equal Protection Clause; whether a course is rigorous enough to be considered "college preparatory" is not a suspect classification, and the policy easily met the rational basis test.

6.1.4. The principle of nondiscrimination

6.1.4.1. Race. In an *en banc* opinion, the U.S. Court of Appeals for the Ninth Circuit reversed the ruling in *Doe v. Kamehameha Schools* (*SA 2d*, p. 287), thus upholding the schools' racially exclusive admissions criteria favoring Native Hawaiian students. The *en banc* opinion, found at 470 F.3d 827 (9th Cir. 2006), first had to resolve what standard of review to use in assessing whether the admissions policy violated 42 U.S.C. Section 1981 (Section 4.5.2.4 of *SA 2d*). The majority determined that the *Weber* test (*SA 2d*, p. 185), created in response to a Title VII challenge to affirmative action in employment, provided an appropriate standard for reviewing claims brought under Section 1981.

Modifying the *Weber* test to fit the educational context of this case, the *en banc* court examined (1) whether there was a manifest imbalance in the educational achievement of the "target population" of Native Hawaiian students; (2) whether the admissions policy "unnecessarily trammeled" the opportunities of the population of nonpreferred students to obtain a satisfactory education; and (3) whether the admissions policy did no more than remedy the imbalance in educational achievement.

The court found a manifest imbalance in the educational attainment of Native Hawaiian students generally. It also found that the nonpreferred group of students performed better, on average, than the target population of Native Hawaiian students, and that the rights of the nonfavored group were not trammeled because their achievement was higher, even if they did not attend the Kamehameha Schools. Third, the majority found that the Schools admit non-Native Hawaiian applicants if there is space available, and that its admissions policy preferences will end when the achievement gap is closed and the imbalance is therefore remedied. Because the preferential admissions policy met all three prongs of the modified Weber test, the *en banc* majority ruled that the policy did not violate Section 1983.

6.1.4.2. Sex. Over the past decade the proportion of women undergraduates has increased at U.S. colleges and universities; in 2006, 57.3 percent of undergraduates were women (U.S. Department of Education, 2009). There is some evidence that private colleges are holding women to somewhat higher standards for admission in an effort to "balance" the proportions of male and female undergraduate students. Although such differences would be unlawful at public colleges under both Title IX and the Equal Protection clause, Title IX contains an exemption for private undergraduate institutions (*SA 2d*, p. 288). Nevertheless, the U.S. Commission on Civil Rights initiated an investigation to ascertain whether such "balancing" is occurring at private liberal arts colleges. Scott Jaschik, "Probe of Extra Help for Men," *Inside Higher Education*, November 2, 2009, available at http://insidehighereducation.com/news/2009/11/02/admit. The investigation was suspended in March of 2011 on the grounds that some colleges had refused to provide data, and there was concern that other data might be "unreliable." "Civil-Rights Panel Suspends Inquiry into Gender Bias in Admissions," *Chron. Higher Educ.*, March 16, 2011, available at http://chronicle.com/blogs/ticker/civil-rights-panel-suspends-inquiry-into-gender-bias-in-admissions/31368.

6.1.4.3. Disability. A case decided by a federal appellate court involving a high school has important implications for colleges and universities that may face claims that an applicant was denied admission because of a disability. In *Ellenberg v. New Mexico Military Academy*, 572 F.3d 815 (10th Cir. 2009), the plaintiff applied for admission to a military high school. She was rejected on the basis of documented prior behavioral problems, prior drug use, and the need for continued medication and counseling. The plaintiff had been classified as disabled under the Individuals with Disabilities Education Act, 20 U.S.C. §1400 *et seq.* (IDEA), a federal law that protects students with disabilities in elementary and secondary education. The plaintiff argued that this classification under the IDEA automatically gave her protection under Section 504 and the ADA. Although the court was willing to believe that the student had a disability, she had not articulated how the alleged disability "substantially limited" her ability to learn, as required by both Section 504 and the ADA. Therefore, the court ruled that simply because an individual qualifies for accommodations under the IDEA, she does not necessarily meet the requirements of the ADA or Section 504, and awarded summary judgment to the defendant school.

6.1.4.4. Immigration status. The Immigration and Customs Enforcement (ICE) division of the Department of Homeland Security has issued a ruling that public colleges and universities may enroll undocumented aliens without violating the law. In a letter responding to an inquiry by the *Raleigh* (NC) *News and Observer,* ICE stated that "it is left to the school to decide whether or not to enroll out-of-status or undocumented nonimmigrants," but warned that these individuals risked "being apprehended and possibly removed from the United States." The letter states:

> The Department of Homeland Security (DHS) does not require any school to
> determine a student's status (i.e., whether or not he or she is legally allowed
> to study). DHS also does not require any school to request immigration status
> information prior to enrolling students or to report to the government if they
> know a student is out of status, except in the case of those who came on student
> visas or for exchange purposes and are registered with the Student Exchange
> and Visitor Program. [available at http://www.news observer.com/content/
> media/2008/5/9/ICE%20statement.pdf]

Sec. 6.1.5. Affirmative action programs. Regarding a rationale for a "differential" affirmative action policy (*SA 2d*, p. 322), controversy has heated up again about the validity of the SAT as applied to the test scores of African American applicants. See, for example, Maria Santelices and Mark Wilson, "The Case of Freedle, the SAT, and the Standardization Approach to Differential Item Functioning," 80 *Harvard Educ. Rev.* 106 (2010).

****

It is still a live issue whether courts applying 42 U.S.C. §1981 (*SA 2d,* sec. 6.1.4.1) to an affirmative action case should always employ standards comparable to those for the equal protection clause (see *SA 2d*, p. 303). In *Doe v. Kamehameha Schools*, 470 F.3d 827 (9th Cir. 2006) (discussed in Section 6.1.4.1 of this *Supplement*), the *en banc* court faced this issue in a case challenging the racially exclusive policy of a private school that received no federal funds. Applying Section 1981, the court utilized Title VII standards (see *SA 2d*, pp. 185–86) in lieu of equal protection standards and upheld the school's policy.

* * * *

Clarification. The references in *SA 2d* to a "race conscious or preferential" affirmative action policy (see p. 323, point 6 and also p. 320, point 3) may suggest that the two phrases are interchangeable. This is apparently no longer the case. In the *Seattle School District* case (*SA 2d*, pp. 314–18), Justice Kennedy used "race conscious" in a way that distinguished it from "preferential," and Chief Justice Roberts apparently did likewise. Both also provided examples of plans that would be "race conscious" but apparently not "preferential." (See discussion of the Kennedy opinion on *SA 2d*, pp. 317–18.)

Sec. 6.2. Financial Aid

6.2.1. General principles. Private entities that make higher education loans to students or their parents are regulated by the Truth in Lending Act, 15 U.S.C. §1601 *et seq.* The Higher Education Opportunity Act, P.L. 110–35 (August 14, 2008), amended the Truth in Lending Act by requiring that creditors obtain a self-certification form signed by the consumer before finalizing the loan and also by requiring creditors that have a preferred lender arrangement with colleges and universities to provide certain information to those institutions. The Federal Reserve Board has published a final rule amending Regulation Z, which implements the Truth in Lending Act. The final rule may be found at 74 *Fed. Reg.* 41194 (August 14, 2009).

6.2.2. Federal programs. The Higher Education Opportunity Act (HEOA), which reauthorized the Higher Education Act of 1965 (and added a number of provisions), was enacted on August 14, 2008. Most but not all of the HEOA's provisions involved federal financial aid programs. For a summary of the provisions of the HEOA, see the "Dear Colleague" letter, which is available at http://ifap.ed.gov/dpcletters/GEN0812FP0810.html.

The National Center for Educational Statistics has published a report, *Information Required to be Disclosed Under the Higher Education Act of 1965: Suggestions for Dissemination* (October 2009), available at http://nces.ed.gov/pubs2010/2010831rev.pdf. The report includes information required to be disclosed under both the Higher Education Act of 1965 and the Higher Education

Opportunity Act of 2008. HEOA additions to required disclosures are highlighted in yellow in the online version of the report.

* * * *

The U.S. Department of Education has published final rules implementing changes to several federal student loan programs resulting from the passage of the HEOA. The final rules apply to Perkins Loans, Federal Family Education Loans, and Direct Loans. Several of the new rules require greater disclosures by institutions to borrowers of their relationships with lenders and guaranty agencies, and the development of institutional codes of conduct related to the institution's participation in the federal student loan program. The final rules are published at 74 Fed. Reg. 55971–56006 (October 29, 2009), and are effective July 1, 2010.

The U.S. Department of Education has also published final rules implementing changes resulting from the enactment of the HEOA to institutional eligibility under the Higher Education Act of 1954, its General Provisions, the Pell Grant and College Work Study programs, the TEACH program, and the LEAP program. Additional rules implementing HEOA requirements are discussed in Section 8.6.3 of this *Supplement.* The final rules are published at 74 Fed. Reg. 55902–55969 (October 29, 2009), and are effective July 1, 2010.

Additional final rules have been published by the U.S. Department of Education that address the integrity of federal student aid programs. The rules address the following issues, which were included in the Higher Education Opportunity Act of 2008; some are addressed to proprietary institutions only, while others apply to all institutions that wish to participate in the federal student aid program. Some of the new requirements are listed below:

> *Issues for proprietary institutions and institutions whose programs do not lead to a degree.* Graduation and job placement rates must be provided to prospective students for every program. The institution must show that each program in which students participate in federal student financial aid programs is either separately accredited or is covered by the institution's accreditation.

> *Issues for all institutions.* The regulations strengthen the Department's authority to take action against institutions engaged in deceptive advertising, marketing, and sales practices. They remove the "safe harbor" provisions that allowed some recruiters to be compensated on their success in enrolling students. They clarify what states must do to authorize an institution to participate in the federal student aid program, and require institutions to verify that a student's high school diploma is valid. The regulations allow students without a high school diploma to participate in federal student aid programs after they complete six credits of college work, and provides that the Department will approve "Ability to Benefit" test materials developed

by testing companies. The regulations require institutions to use a "structured and consistent approach" to determining whether a student is making satisfactory academic progress, and streamline the process for student verification of the information on their Free Application for Federal Student Aid (FAFSA) (the latter is effective July 1, 2012). They also state the metric for determining the definition of a "credit hour," and impose new requirements on institutions that deliver a portion of another institution's educational program.

These final rules are found at 75 Fed. Reg. 66832–66975 and 75 Fed. Reg. 66665–66677 (October 29, 2010), and most are effective July 1, 2011.

* * * *

A legal challenge to a provision in the Higher Education Act, 20 U.S.C.S. §1091(r), which denies federal student aid for one year to individuals who have received federal student aid and have been convicted of possessing a controlled substance, for two years for those convicted twice, and permanently to those convicted three times, has been rejected. The law provides that the ineligibility period may be shortened for those students who have successfully demonstrated their rehabilitation in compliance with the law's guidelines. In *Students for Sensible Drug Policy Foundation v. Spellings*, 523 F.3d 896 (8th Cir. 2008), the appellate court affirmed the trial court's rejection of the students' claim that the denial of student aid violated the Fifth Amendment of the U.S. Constitution's Double Jeopardy Clause because it punished the student twice for the same offense. The court used a two-step analysis to determine whether the penalty was civil, which would not be a violation, or criminal, which could violate the Double Jeopardy Clause. First, the court examined whether the intent of the provision was remedial or to deter certain conduct. The court found several remedial purposes for the provision, including its purpose to increase access to postsecondary education, to encourage drug rehabilitation, and that it rewarded law-abiding students. Second, the court found that the provision was not punitive because it was not a permanent deprivation, it did not rely on an intent to violate the law, which made it unlike a criminal statute, and is rationally related to a number of remedial purposes, as discussed above.

* * * *

The attempt of a student to avoid repaying his federal Stafford Loan was rejected by a California appellate court. In *Davies v. Sallie Mae, Inc.*, 2008 Cal. App. Unpub. LEXIS 8616 (Cal. App. 1 Dist., 2008, Oct. 31, 2008), the plaintiff sued Sallie Mae, challenging its decision to place the loan in default. Davies had graduated from law school and took a job with an attorney who did not pay him, with the exception of a small amount for room and board, because the cases on which he was working were contingent fee cases and had not yet been resolved. Therefore, Davies was unable to repay his loan obligation.

Davies' employer had written several letters to Sallie Mae substantiating Davies' economic situation. Davies claimed that that letter was a contract to which he was a third-party beneficiary. He also claimed that the promissory note that he signed was defective and that he should receive equitable relief from the requirement that the loan be repaid immediately under the theory of changed circumstances, impossibility, extrinsic fraud, equitable estoppels, and laches.

The court ruled that Davies' claims were really challenges to regulations under the Higher Education Act and thus he had no cause of action, since there is no private right of action under the Higher Education Act. Furthermore, said the court, the letters from his employer did not create a contract. Therefore, the court affirmed the trial court's dismissal of all claims for failure to state a claim for which relief may be given.

6.2.4. Affirmative action in financial aid programs

Clarification. If an affirmative action financial aid policy were challenged using Section 1981 (*SA 2d*, p. 338), it is not entirely clear that the court would apply the equal protection strict scrutiny standard of review (*SA 2d*, p. 340). In *Doe v. Kamehameha Schools*, 470 F.3d 827 (9th Cir. 2006) (see Section 6.1.5 of this *Supplement*), the *en banc* court applied Title VII standards, rather than equal protection standards, to a racially exclusive admissions policy of a private school that did not receive federal funds.

6.2.5. Discrimination against nonresidents

Clarifications. Shim v. Rutgers, the State University, 924 A.2d 465 (N.J. 2007) (*SA 2d*, p. 347) also provides a helpful illustration of the interpretation of administrative regulations. The university relied on a regulation (N.J.A.C. 9A: 5–11(f)) to support its position that, if a student is financially dependent on her parents, her domicile remains that of the parents. According to the court, this administrative regulation created a *presumption* against domicile for a student who is financially dependent on out-of-state parents. In contrast, the statute that the student relied on (N.J.S.A. 18A: 62–4) created a *presumption* in favor of domicile for a student who has been resident in the state for at least a year. Reading the statute together with the regulation, the New Jersey Supreme Court determined that the administrative regulation's presumption and the statute's presumption in effect "neutralized" each other. In such circumstances, "Rutgers must then fully, fairly, and dispassionately consider *all* submitted evidence" and determine by "a preponderance of the evidence [whether] the student's domicile is in New Jersey."

* * * *

In the state administrative law context (*SA 2d*, pp. 347–48), issues may also occasionally arise about whether a public university's residency decisions are subject to the state's administrative procedure act. See, e.g., *George Mason University v. Floyd*, 654 S.E. 2d 556 (Va. 2008) (residency decisions not subject to state Administrative Process Act).

6.2.6. *Discrimination against aliens*

6.2.6.2. *Undocumented aliens.* An official of the U.S. Immigration and Customs Enforcement office (ICE) has clarified the issue of whether state colleges and universities may admit undocumented aliens as students. In a letter to a state official in North Carolina, the ICE official explained that Section 1621 of the Illegal Immigration Reform and Immigrant Responsibility Act (IIRIRA) does not regulate admission to a public college or university, but only prohibits giving such aliens "benefits" such as financial aid. (Letter from J. Pendergraph to T. Ziko, July 9, 2008, available at www.nacua.org in the Legal Resources section.)

****

Some states are passing laws allowing undocumented students to qualify for in-state tuition rates, while other states are passing laws that prohibit undocumented aliens from qualifying, on the basis of residency, for financial aid or in-state tuition rates. (See, for example, S. Car. Stats. §59–101–430(B).) Court challenges to both types of laws are arising. For information and citations on such legislation, in addition to the sources in *SA 2d* (p. 355), go to http://www.ncsl.org/progams/immig/immig_InStateTuition0808.htm (Web site of the National Conference of State Legislatures). For further updating and analysis, see Michael Olivas, "The Political Economy of the DREAM Act and the Legislative Process: A Case Study of Comprehensive Immigration Reform," 55 *Wayne Law Rev.* 1757, 1759–1788 (2009); and Sharon Senghor, "Undocumented Students and the DREAM Act: Subsequent Developments and Trends," in *NACUANotes* Vol. 8, No. 10 (May 28, 2010). (*Note:* The most recent version of the federal DREAM Act, discussed in both these articles, was defeated in Congress as this *Supplement* was going to press.)

****

In the leading case to date, *Martinez v. Regents of the University of California*, 241 P.3d 855(Cal. 2010), the Supreme Court of California upheld a state law that provides in-state tuition rates for some undocumented students. The case illustrates the potential conflicts between such laws and federal immigration laws (see *SA 2d*, p. 355) and demonstrates one way in which courts may resolve such potential conflicts. The California law at issue exempts undocumented aliens (and others) from paying nonresident tuition if they had attended California high schools for at least three years and meet certain other requirements (Cal. Ed. Code §68130.5). Federal law, however, prohibits states from making undocumented aliens eligible for postsecondary education benefits on the basis of state residency unless U.S. citizens and permanent residents are also eligible for these benefits (8 U.S.C. §1623; see *SA 2d*, p. 354). The plaintiffs in *Martinez* argued (primarily) that the California statute violated the federal statute and was therefore invalid. The state Supreme Court determined otherwise:

> . . . The question is whether the exemption in the state statute is based on residence within California in violation of [8 U.S.C.] section 1623. Because

the exemption is given to all who have attended high school in California for at least three years (and meet the other requirements), and not all who have done so qualify as California residents for purposes of in-state tuition, and further because not all unlawful aliens who would qualify as residents but for their unlawful status are eligible for the exemption, we conclude the exemption is not based on residence in California. Rather, it is based on other criteria. Accordingly, section 68130.5 does not violate section 1623. [241 P.3d at 860.]

The California Supreme Court therefore reversed the judgment of the California Court of Appeal (83 Cal. Rptr. 3d 518) that had invalidated the state statute, in part on grounds that the federal law "preempted" the state law.

* * * *

For a Web site providing advice for student affairs professionals on advising undocumented students, and an overview of pertinent state and federal legal developments, go to http://professionals.collegeboard.com/guidance/financial-aid/undocumented-students.

Selected Annotated Bibliography

Sec. 6.1. (Admissions)

Alger, Jonathan R. "From Desegregation to Diversity and Beyond: Our Evolving Legal Conversation on Race and Higher Education." 36 *J. Coll. & Univ. Law* 983 (2010). Reviews the legal rationales over fifty years involving the consideration of race in higher education admissions and reflects on lessons learned "from this ongoing conversation about moral and educational issues" related to affirmative action.

Connell, Mary Ann. "Race and Higher Education: The Tortuous Journey Toward Desegregation." 36 *J. Coll. & Univ. Law* 945 (2010). Traces the history of *de jure* and *de facto* segregation in public higher education, and litigation, from cases prior to *Brown v. Board of Education* through recent settlements of long-term desegregation cases in Mississippi, Louisiana, Tennessee, and Alabama.

Symposium, "Law, Ethics, and Affirmative Action in America, 78 *U. Cinn. L. Rev.* 873 (2004). An interdisciplinary collection of articles focusing on the ramifications of the *Grutter* and *Gratz* cases. See especially, Joseph Tomain, "Introduction"; Ronald Dworkin, "The Court and the University"; Marvin Krislow, "Affirmative Action in Higher Education: the Value, the Method, and the Future"; and Paul Boudreaux, "Diversity and Democracy."

Sec. 6.2. (Financial Aid)

Bruno, Andorra. "Unauthorized Alien Students: Issues and 'DREAM Act' Legislation." Congressional Research Report for Congress, No. RL33863 (January 8, 2009), available at http://web.mit.edu/kolya/.f/root/net.mit.edu/sipb.mit.edu/contrib/wikileaks-crs/wikileaks-crs-reports/RL33863.pdf. Provides background on the DREAM Act legislation and its current status.

Felder, Jody. "Unauthorized Alien Students, Higher Education, and In-State Tuition Rates: A Legal Analysis." Congressional Research Report for Congress No. RS22500

(October 7, 2008), available at http://www.house.gov/gallegly/issues/immigration/imdocs/RS22500.pdf. Reviews cases involving access by undocumented students to public higher education and state laws making in-state tuition available to undocumented aliens.

Flores, Stella M. "State Dream Acts: The Effect of In-State Resident Tuition Policies and Undocumented Latino Students." 33 *Review of Higher Education* 239 (2010). Uses Current Population Survey data to estimate the effect of in-state tuition policies for undocumented Latino students; concludes that such policies in those states that have adopted them significantly increases the number of undocumented Latino students who enroll in college.

Olivas, Michael. "The DREAM Act and In-State Tuition for Undocumented Students," in B. Lauren (ed.), *The College Admissions Officer's Guide* (Am. Ass'n of Collegiate Registrars and Admissions Officers, 2008). Frames the issues regarding undocumented applicants and students that are most important for admissions and financial aid officers; and reviews and analyzes pertinent state legislation, federal legislation, court cases, and state attorney general opinions.

7

The Campus Community

Sec. 7.1. Student Housing

7.1.1. Housing regulations. Students with disabilities may request accommodations that involve exceptions to an institution's housing policies. Such was the case in *Fialka-Feldman v. Oakland University Board of Trustees*, 678 F. Supp. 2d 576 (E.D. Mich. 2009). The plaintiff, a student with cognitive disabilities, was enrolled at the university in a non-credit continuing education program. He applied to live in on-campus housing, but his application was denied because he was not enrolled in a degree-granting program, which was required by the university's housing policy. The plaintiff sued under the Fair Housing Act, the Americans with Disabilities Act, and Section 504 of the Rehabilitation Act. The plaintiff later dropped his claim under the Fair Housing Act.

The university defended its policy, stating that the plaintiff was not a "qualified" student with a disability because he was not enrolled in a degree-granting program. The plaintiff argued that it was his cognitive disability that prevented him from pursuing a degree, and therefore the disability itself was the reason he was not permitted to live in campus housing. Although the university argued that allowing non-degree students to live in campus housing would defeat the academic purpose of such housing, the court characterized the plaintiff's request as a waiver of the housing policy for him alone rather than a change to the housing policy for all non-degree students. The court concluded that the university's refusal to engage in the interactive process required by the ADA and Section 504 violated these laws, and awarded summary judgment to the plaintiff. The court awarded summary judgment to the university on the plaintiff's disparate treatment claim, noting that he had been denied campus housing not because of his disability, but because of his enrollment status. The university has appealed the summary judgment ruling.

A federal trial court addressed the issue of when a student's claim of disability discrimination in housing begins to run: when a housing unit is completed and ready for occupancy, or when the student agrees to rent a housing unit from the institution. In *Kuchmas v. Towson University*, 553 F. Supp. 2d 556 (D. Md. 2008), a disabled student sued the university and the design and construction firm responsible for developing an apartment complex that the university used to house students, including students with disabilities. The student alleged that the unit was not "accessible" as had been represented to him, and he could not use the shower and other facilities in the apartment. The university argued that the statute of limitations had expired and the student's lawsuit was untimely. The court ruled that, because the university had a continuing responsibility to provide accessible housing to students with disabilities, the statute of limitations began to run when the student signed the rental agreement, not when the housing unit first became available for rental.

Although many institutions include gender identity and expression in their nondiscrimination policies, they have been slow to address the special housing needs of transgender students. Some of the issues that institutions are finding it necessary to address are gender-neutral bathrooms, whether the institution will allow individuals of different biological sexes to room together, and other issues related to the separation of students by their biological sex but not necessarily their gender. For a thoughtful discussion of some of these issues, see Alexandra Tilsley, "New Policies Accommodate Transgender Students." *Chron. Higher Educ.*, June 27, 2010, available at http://chronicle.com/article/Colleges-Rewrite-Rules-to/66046/. See also Katherine A. Womack, Comment: "Please Check One—Male or Female?: Confronting Gender Identity Discrimination in Collegiate Residential Life." 44 *Univ. of Richmond Law Rev.* 1365 (2010).

* * * *

What is the responsibility—and potential legal liability—of an institution when a nonstudent who resides on campus engages in harassing or discriminatory behavior toward a student (or employee)? The New Jersey Supreme Court addressed that issue in *Godfrey v. Princeton Theological Seminary*, 952 A.2d 1034 (N.J. 2008). In *Godfrey*, two students at a private, religiously affiliated institution sued the seminary under both Title IX (see *SA 2d*, pp. 735–38) and the New Jersey Law Against Discrimination, which forbids discrimination on the basis of sex in places of public accommodation. The students alleged that a tenant who lived in one of the seminary's housing units on campus, who was neither a student nor an employee, had stalked them, attempted to coerce them into a social relationship, and engaged in other behaviors that were annoying and bothersome. The students argued that the seminary had not responded appropriately to their complaints, first telling them that it was a police matter and not the seminary's responsibility, and later warning them that they could be liable for defamation if they persisted in complaining about the tenant's behavior to seminary authorities.

The court did not address whether the state nondiscrimination law's definition of "place of public accommodation" applied to a religiously affiliated entity, although the law specifically excludes any "educational facility operated or maintained by a bona fide religious or sectarian institution" (N.J. Stat. §10:5–5(l)), because the trial and appellate courts had determined that the behavior complained of by the students did not meet the "severe or pervasive" requirement of the court's earlier jurisprudence on sexual harassment. The trial and appellate courts had also found that the seminary's response to the students' complaints was not deliberately indifferent, and thus their Title IX claim failed as well. The state supreme court did, however, comment that had the behavior been more severe, or more pervasive, liability might have been found, and criticized the seminary for what the court perceived as an inadequate response to the students' concerns.

Counsel might consider reviewing their institution's policy against harassment to ensure that it applies to harassment of a student or employee by individuals who are not students or employees, but who are on campus because of either a relationship with a student (for example, a student's spouse or partner living in on-campus housing) or because they are a vendor or independent contractor. Other types of individuals whose behavior might cause liability for institutions include individuals attending summer or winter break programs (such as programs for alumni) or guest lecturers who are housed on campus during their visit. The defendant in *Godfrey* appeared reluctant to take action against the alleged harasser because he was neither a student nor an employee; under both Title IX and state nondiscrimination laws, this may not be an adequate defense to a claim of harassment.

7.1.2. *Searches and seizures.*

Searches of residence hall rooms at private colleges and universities continue to pose difficult issues with respect to the application of the Fourth Amendment to such searches. Although a state appellate court ruled that a warrantless search by police officers at Boston College did not violate a student's Fourth Amendment rights, the state's highest court reversed that ruling and stated that the evidence obtained during the search could not be used. In *Commonwealth v. Carr*, 918 N.E.2d 847 (Mass. App. Ct. 2009), *rev'd*, 2010 Mass. LEXIS 871 (Mass. November 17, 2010), a resident advisor had contacted campus police because two students had told her that they had seen a student with a knife and believed that his roommate had a gun. Boston College's housing policy forbids weapons in the residence halls, and also reserved the right to inspect students' rooms for safety reasons. The campus police went to the room, asked the student for the gun and other weapons, and were handed a plastic replica gun and two knives. The police then asked the students for permission to search the room, although neither student consented to the search in writing. The police found several types of unlawful drugs during the search.

Although a trial court ruled that the drug evidence must be suppressed because the students had not consented to the search, the appellate court disagreed. Because Boston College is private, said the court, the police officers' conduct did not violate the Fourth Amendment. The court characterized the officers' conduct as furthering the interests of their private employer in investigating to ascertain whether the housing policy were being violated by the students' possession of weapons.

But the Supreme Judicial Court of Massachusetts rejected that reasoning. It ruled that the trial judge had ruled appropriately, and did not address the appellate court's discussion of whether the Fourth Amendment should apply to a search by police of a private college residence hall room.

Sec. 7.2. Campus Computer Networks

7.2.1. Freedom of speech.

In *State v. Drahota*, 788 N.W. 2d 796 (Neb. 2010), the Nebraska Supreme Court considered whether the "fighting words" exception could apply to e-mails (see *SA 2d*, p. 374 fn. 2). Drahota had sent the e-mails, anonymously, to a former professor of his, at his university e-mail address. The e-mails were "laced with provocative and insulting rhetoric and—with the Iraq war as a background—suggested that [the professor] was a traitor and that he sympathized with Al Qaeda." After law enforcement authorities had identified Drahota as the author of the e-mails and charged him with breach of the peace, Drahota claimed that his e-mails were protected by the First Amendment.

The state argued that the e-mails were unprotected fighting words. Relying on *Chaplinsky v. New Hampshire*, 315 U.S. 568 (1942), the Nebraska Supreme Court disagreed. It held that a speaker cannot be punished "under the fighting words exception solely because [the speech] inflicts emotional injury, annoys, offends, or angers another person." It is, rather, "the tendency or likelihood of the words to provoke violent reaction that is the touchstone" of the exception (788 N.W. 2d at 656, quoting *Lemar v. Banks*, 684 F.2d at 718 (11th Cir. 1982)). Thus,

> [E]ven if a fact finder could conclude that in a face-to-face confrontation, Drahota's speech would have provoked an immediate retaliation, [the professor] could not have immediately retaliated. [He] did not know who sent the e-mails, let alone where to find the author. [788 N.W. 2d at 638.]

7.2.2. Liability issues.

The case of *Murakowski v. University of Delaware*, 575 F. Supp. 2d 571 (D. Del. 2008), illustrates the application of the true threat exception (*SA 2d*, pp. 374–75) to campus regulation of student cyber speech. It also illustrates how the *Tinker* "material and substantial disruption" standard (*SA 2d*, Sec. 10.1, pp.479–80) may be used in analyzing the validity of campus regulations of student cyber speech. *Murakowski* concerned a student's free speech challenge to university discipline imposed for maintaining, on a university server, a personal Web site that university officials considered to be "graphic in nature, violent, derogatory, hostile, and disturbing." The court first applied the true threat doctrine, determining that the Web site's content did not constitute a true threat, and thus rejecting the university's first argument for upholding its disciplinary action even though it was based on the content of the student's speech. The court then applied the *Tinker* standard, determining that the university had not proven that the Web site's content created the disruption of campus life, and thus rejecting the university's second argument for upholding its disciplinary action.

* * * *

The case of *United States v. Heckenkamp*, 482 F.3d 1142 (9th Cir. 2007), suggests other potential liabilities of colleges and universities under the Fourth Amendment. The case concerns a federal prosecution of a graduate student in computer science at the University of Wisconsin/Madison, brought under the Computer Fraud and Abuse Act (18 U.S.C. §1030, as amended). The student defendant challenged the prosecution as violating the Fourth Amendment's search and seizure provisions. Although it was a government prosecution backed by the FBI, the primary issues concerned searches of the student's personal computer by university personnel. The student was suspected of using his personal computer, attached to the university network, to "hack" into (or gain unauthorized access to) the network of a private corporation. A computer system administrator for the corporation determined that the hacker had used a computer on the University of Wisconsin at Madison's network, and contacted the university's computer department. In response, a university network investigator examined the situation, finding evidence that a computer on the university network had hacked into the corporation's system and that the computer user had gained unauthorized access to the university's e-mail server. He traced the source of intrusion to a specific IP address located in university housing and determined that the student (Heckenkamp), and no one else, checked his e-mail from this IP address before the unauthorized access to the company's and the university's systems was established.

The university network investigator then took various steps to protect the university's e-mail server and network, and to gather further facts; he also contacted the FBI and university police. One of the actions he took—at night and working from home—came to be known in the later criminal prosecution as the "remote search." Checking the network, he determined that the student's personal computer was no longer connected to the network through the original IP address, but that it was connected through a different IP address. To verify this conclusion, the investigator then "logged into the computer, using a name and password he had discovered in his earlier investigation. . . . [He] used a series of commands to confirm that the computer was the same [one] and to determine whether the computer still posed a risk to the university server. After approximately 15 minutes of looking only in the temporary directory, without deleting, modifying, or destroying any files, [the investigator] logged off of the computer" (482 F.3d at 1145).[1]

---

[1]Subsequently, the network administrator and university police entered the student's dormitory room (without consent) and conducted a search of his computer. The court made no ruling on the constitutionality of this search. The analysis is complicated by university police having located the student, who then provided his password at the officer's request, and also then consented to the network investigator's request to make a copy of the computer's hard drive.

Regarding this "remote search," the court first held that the student "had a legitimate, objectively reasonable expectation of privacy in his personal computer." It then considered "whether the student defendant's objectively reasonable expectation of privacy in his computer was eliminated when he attached it to the university network." It was not: "the mere act of accessing a network does not in itself extinguish privacy expectations, nor does the fact that others may have occasional access to the computer." "However, privacy expectations may be reduced if the user is advised that information transmitted through the network is not confidential and that the systems administrators may monitor communications transmitted by the user." And a "person's reasonable expectation of privacy may be diminished in transmissions over the Internet or e-mail that have already arrived at the recipient" (quoting *United States v. Lifshitz*, 369 F.3d 173, 190 (2d Cir. 2004)). (See *Heckenkamp*, 482 F.3d at 1146–47.)

Applying these guidelines, the court determined that the university had "no announced monitoring policy on the network" and, to the contrary, provided substantial privacy protection to computer network users, except in narrow circumstances in which university access to private computers is "essential to . . . protect the integrity of the University and the rights and property of the state" (quoting policy). "Thus university computer policies [did] not eliminate [the student's] expectation of privacy. . . ." Rather, "he retained an objectively reasonable expectation of privacy in his personal computer, which was protected by a screen-saver password, located in his dormitory room, and subject to no policy allowing the university actively to monitor or audit his computer usage."

This conclusion, however, did not mean that the student prevailed on his Fourth Amendment privacy claim. Instead, the court went on to consider whether there were any special circumstances that would justify the university network investigator's remote search of computer files on the student's hard drive, done without a warrant and without the student's consent. In particular, the court considered whether the search of the computer was justified under what is called the "special needs" exception to the warrant requirement—an exception that may apply if "special needs, beyond the normal need for law enforcement, make the warrant and probable-cause requirement impracticable."

In applying this exception, the court emphasized that the university investigator had acted to secure the university's e-mail server and not "to collect evidence for law enforcement purposes or at the request of law enforcement agents." Moreover, the "integrity and security of the campus e-mail system was in jeopardy," and the administrator "needed to act immediately to protect the system." The remote search, moreover, was "remarkably limited" in scope, such that the intrusion into the student's privacy was outweighed by the "university's interest in . . . determining the source" of the threat to the security of its network.

The court thus concluded that, "although the student had a reasonable expectation of privacy in his personal computer, the [warrantless remote] search of the computer was justified under the 'special needs' exception to the warrant requirement."

Sec. 7.3. Campus Security

7.3.1. Security officers. The Supreme Court of Montana has ruled that an off-campus traffic stop made by a University of Montana security officer was a valid exercise of his authority and has refused to suppress evidence of driving while intoxicated. In *State v. Howard*, 184 P.3d 344 (Mont. 2008), the court examined a memorandum of understanding entered by the University of Montana, the city police department, and the county sheriff's office. The memorandum gave university security officers authority within the boundaries of the campus, over an area within one mile of the exterior boundaries of the campus, and over other property owned, controlled, or administered by the university. Finding that the traffic stop occurred within the area covered by the memorandum, the court ruled that the security officer had the requisite authority and refused to suppress the evidence of the driver's intoxication. For a case using similar reasoning to reach the same outcome, see *State v. Hardgrove*, 225 P.3d 357 (Wash. Ct. App. 2010).

But the Supreme Court of Massachusetts refused to recognize the lawfulness of the arrest and ensuing search of an individual prosecuted for possession of controlled substances. In *Commonwealth v. Hernandez*, 924 N.E.2d 709 (Mass. 2010), two Boston University police, acting as "special state police officers" under Massachusetts law, had stopped an individual after running a check of the individual's car registration and learning that a warrant had been issued for a motor vehicle violation. The individual had not committed an offense on university property, nor did the officers stop him for any offense that they had observed. The officers arrested the individual, had him transported to the Boston University police department, and searched his car; heroin and cocaine were found in the car. The court ruled that the evidence must be suppressed because the university police did not have the authority to execute an arrest warrant because the arrest did not occur on university property and the underlying crime for which the warrant had been issued had not occurred within the jurisdiction of the university.

* * * *

Campus police at private colleges and universities may be viewed by courts as "state actors" if they have powers to arrest or other forms of authority derived from being commissioned by local government as police officers. For example, in *Maniaci v. Georgetown University*, 510 F. Supp. 2d 50 (D.D.C. 2007), campus police at Georgetown, a private university, removed a conference attendee from a building after he disrupted the proceedings, and he was injured in the process of that removal. He sued the university, claiming that his constitutional rights were violated by the Georgetown campus police. The court, noting that Georgetown's campus police are commissioned as "special police" by the Washington, D.C. police department and have the power of arrest, rejected the university's motion for summary judgment on the constitutional claim, stating that if the plaintiff could prove his allegations that the campus police had detained him and prevented him from leaving, such actions were incident to a potential arrest and could thus form the basis for a finding that the campus police had engaged in state action because their arrest power came from the city.

For further discussion of the interplay between state action and security officers with respect to residence hall searches, see *SA 2d*, Section 7.1.2 and the same section in this *Supplement*. For more general discussion of the state action doctrine, including analysis of another recent security officer case (*Limpuangthip v. United States*), see *SA 2d*, Section 1.5.2 and the same section in this *Supplement*.

7.3.2. *Protecting students against violent crime.* A state appellate court ruled that the University of Cincinnati was not liable for the rape of a student in a residence hall bathroom. In *Shivers v. University of Cincinnati*, 2006 Ohio 5518 (Ohio Ct. App. 2006), a female student alleged that the university had provided insufficient security for the residence hall, in particular, that there were no locks on the bathroom doors. Although the trial court had found for the plaintiff, the appellate court reversed, ruling that the assault was not foreseeable. A previous rape that had occurred in a different building located at some distance from the residence hall and occurring two years earlier was not close enough in time or location to suggest that the assault in the bathroom was foreseeable, according to the appellate court.

* * * *

The question of whether or not to perform background checks on applicants for admission is troublesome, and a recent court ruling provides no reassurance on that matter. A federal trial court addressed the issue of protecting students from violence from their peers in *Estate of Levi Butler v. Maharishi University of Management*, 589 F. Supp. 2d 1150 (D. Iowa 2008). Butler was stabbed by a fellow student in a campus building and died of his wounds. Earlier on the day of the stabbing, the assailant had attacked another student, who was injured but survived. Although university officials were aware of the attack, they did not call security or report the attack to the police. After the first attack, the dean of men assumed charge of the assailant, spent some time with him, and then returned him to campus where he mingled with other students and committed the second attack that resulted in Butler's death. Butler's father sued Maharishi University of Management (MUM) for premises liability, fraudulent misrepresentation, and negligence. MUM filed a motion for summary judgment on the second and third claims, which the court denied.

The plaintiff had stated that recruiting materials from MUM stressed its peaceful environment and its focus on transcendental meditation, stating that the campus was safe and free from violence. The campus safety policy also stated that MUM officials worked closely with campus security and local police forces. The court found that the existence of these materials, and the potential that Butler relied on their representations, could support a claim of fraudulent misrepresentation, particularly because officials did not report the earlier assault to either security or the police. For similar reasons, the court rejected the defendant's motion for summary judgment on the negligent misrepresentation claim. And with respect to the plaintiff's claim of negligent admission of the assailant, the court referred to testimony that the assailant had told an admissions officer that he had been "arrested a few times," but that there was no investigation into the nature of the charges against the assailant or any attempt to ascertain whether he had mental health problems. At the time of the assaults, the assailant had stopped taking his medication for schizophrenia, and after he was admitted, he told a doctor at the university's student health center that he had previously suffered a "nervous breakdown." In light of the school's failure to investigate the nature of the assailant's criminal record and its failure to gather additional information about his mental status once it was aware of a previous problem, said the court, summary judgment on the negligent admission claim was inappropriate.

7.3.3. Federal statutes and campus security. Final rules for additional information disclosure and security policies enacted in the Higher Education Opportunity Act of 2008 have been published at 74 Fed. Reg. 55902–55969 (October 29, 2009). They include requirements that institutions that provide on-campus housing facilities develop and make available a missing student notification policy, expand the list of crimes that institutions must include in the hate crimes statistics submitted to the Department of Education, and include in their annual security report a statement of emergency response and evacuation procedures.

Sec. 7.4. Other Support Services

7.4.2. Health services. The 2009 Health Information Technology for Economic and Clinical Health Act (HITECH Act), P. L. 111–5, Div. A, Title XIII, will have a substantial impact on the application of HIPAA (the Health Insurance Portability and Accountability Act) to colleges and universities (see *SA 2d*, p. 391). The HITECH Act enlarges the range of health services activities—of higher education institutions as well as health care entities, such as county and state government mental health agencies, with whom institutions have dealings—that potentially could become subject to HIPAA. The HITECH Act also, among other things, imposes new privacy and security requirements on entities subject to the Act. See generally Barbara Bennett, Alexander Dreier, and Candace Martin, "HITECH Act: New Law Requires Significant Investment in Health Information Privacy and Security," NACUANOTES, vol. 7, no.9 (Nat'l Ass'n of College & Univ. Attys., 2009).

Selected Annotated Bibliography

Sec. 7.3. (Campus Security)

Jacobson, Jeffrey S. *Campus Police Authority: Understanding Your Police Officers' Territorial Jurisdiction*. (Nat'l Assn. of College & Univ. Attys., 2006). Discusses the scope of campus officers' territorial authority and various methods that can be used to expand that jurisdiction if advisable. Includes recent court cases and addresses questions concerning what campus police agencies can or should do; also discusses potential liability of officers and institutions for unauthorized actions by campus police.

Sec. 7.4. (Other Support Services)

Bianchi, Melissa. *The HIPAA Privacy Regulations and Student Health Centers.* (Nat'l Ass'n of College & Univ. Attys., 2006). Focuses on the HIPAA privacy regulations, including their interaction with FERPA, and their applicability to student health centers, and it delineates the options for structuring an institution's student health center policies to ensure their compliance with the Privacy Rule.

8

Academic Policies and Concerns

Sec. 8.2. Awarding of Grades and Degrees

A state appellate court has affirmed a trial court's rejection of a student's attempt to claim a breach of contract in a grade dispute. In *Keefe v. New York Law School*, 897 N.Y.S. 2d 94 (N.Y. App. Div. 2010), the student had transferred from another law school and claimed that he was disadvantaged because the law school refused to allow a pass/fail grade to be given in his legal writing class. The student sought a court order to require the law school to change its grading system. Not surprisingly, the trial court dismissed his claim, saying that there was no implied contract to grade him on a pass/fail basis, and the student handbook explicitly stated that letter grades would be used.

* * * *

Two trial courts have rejected claims of students that their constitutional rights of free speech, free exercise of religion, due process and equal protection rights were violated by the requirements of master's programs in counseling that students set aside their religious and moral beliefs when counseling clients. In *Ward v. Wilbanks*, 2010 WL 3026428 (E.D. Mich. 7/26/10), the plaintiff had been dismissed from a master's program in counseling and sought summary judgment against the university. In *Keeton v. Anderson-Wiley*, 733 F. Supp. 2d 1368 (S.D. Ga. 2010), the plaintiff sought a preliminary injunction to keep the graduate program in counseling from requiring her to meet certain academic requirements. Both rulings are reminders of how important it is that faculty and program administrators have clear academic requirements based upon appropriate pedagogical goals.

In *Ward*, the master's program in counseling required students to complete a clinical "practicum" that involved counseling actual clients. The student handbook and the program curriculum referenced the American Counseling

65

Association's code of ethics, and the program was required to ensure that students understood and adhered to that code of ethics as a condition of the program's accreditation. The plaintiff, Julea Ward, espoused religious beliefs that viewed homosexuality as a sin. When she was assigned to counsel a client who had expressed concerns about his sexual orientation in previous counseling sessions, Ward attempted to transfer the client to a different counselor because she disapproved of his sexual orientation. This request triggered an "informal review" by two of Ward's professors, who criticized her refusal to counsel the client and reminded her that the code of ethics requires counselors to set aside their personal values or beliefs and work constructively with the client. They developed a "remediation plan" for Ward that included readings on the psychology of sexual orientation and following the code of ethics' requirements that counselors respect the values of the clients. Ward refused to comply with the remediation plan and requested a formal hearing. After a formal hearing before several program faculty, at which Ward refused to promise to change her behavior, the program faculty decided to dismiss her from the program.

Ward sued the program faculty and the university, asserting that her dismissal violated her free speech rights, free exercise of religion rights, and establishment clause rights under the First Amendment. She characterized the program's requirements as a "speech code" and argued that the requirement that she set aside her religious beliefs while counseling a client constituted "compelled speech." The university, on the other hand, argued that Ward was dismissed for violating the counselors' code of ethics, not because of her religious beliefs.

The court reviewed the program's academic requirements as well as the information included in the Student Handbook. The Student Handbook specified grounds for taking disciplinary action against a student in the counseling program.

> Academic disciplinary action may be initiated when a student exhibits the
> following behavior in one discrete episode that is a violation of law or of the
> ACA Code of Ethics and/or when a student exhibits a documented pattern of
> recurring behavior which may include, but is not limited to . . . [u]nethical,
> threatening, or unprofessional conduct; . . . [c]onsistent inability or unwillingness
> to carry out academic or field placement responsibilities; . . . inability to tolerate
> different points of view, constructive feedback or supervision.

The court also examined course texts and the language of the code of ethics; all of these sources required students to counsel clients without regard to the counselor's own moral, ethical, or religious beliefs.

The court rejected Ward's claim that the code of ethics was a speech code and characterized it as a curricular requirement. This was an important distinction, as courts tend to defer to curricular decisions, but have frequently found that speech codes at public colleges and universities do not pass constitutional muster (see *SA 2d*, Section 10.2).

With respect to Ward's free speech claim, the court relied on *Hazelwood* (*SA 2d*, pp. 554–55) and *Axson-Flynn* (*SA 2d*, pp. 257–60) and determined that the program's inclusion of the code of ethics was "reasonably related to legitimate pedagogical concerns," and not compelled speech. Similarly, the court rejected Ward's claim that the program faculty tried to change her religious beliefs, stating that the evidence did not support that claim. The court also rejected Ward's establishment clause claim, evaluating it under the three-prong *Lemon* test (*SA 2d*, pp. 46–47) and concluding that the curricular requirement of complying with the counselors' code of ethics had a secular purpose, neither advanced nor inhibited religion, and did not entangle the public institution and its program with religion. The court awarded summary judgment to the university on all counts.

Less than a month after the decision in *Ward*, a federal trial court in Georgia issued its decision in *Keeton v. Anderson-Wiley* (above). The plaintiff, a master's student in a counseling program at Augusta State University, had religious beliefs about homosexuality that, she claimed, precluded her from counseling homosexual clients. She asserted these beliefs in course papers, in classroom discussions, and in discussions with fellow students and with professors. As a result of her statements, the program faculty determined that she would be placed on "remediation" status, which included reading psychological research about sexual orientation and its causes and research about the lack of success of "conversion therapy," which Keeton had embraced as a strategy for "converting" clients into heterosexuals. Keeton refused to follow the remediation plan, and sought a preliminary injunction to prevent the program from dismissing her. She made the same Constitutional claims that Ward had recited in her lawsuit.[1]

The court began its analysis of Keeton's claims by stating that "the Supreme Court and the Eleventh Circuit have held that matters of educational policy should be left to educators and it is not the proper role of federal judges to second guess an educator's professional judgment" (2010 U.S. Dist. LEXIS 85959 at *17), citing *Martinez* (discussed in this *Supplement* in Section 11.1.4), *Hazelwood* (*SA 2d*, pp. 554–55), and *Ewing* (*SA 2d*, pp. 76–77). Noting the similarity of the case before it to *Ward*, the court analyzed Keeton's claims in much the same way that the *Ward* court had dealt with her claims. The court viewed the faculty's requirement that Keeton complete the remediation plan as an academic requirement, rather than compelled speech or interference with her religious beliefs, and denied the motion for a preliminary injunction.

In both *Ward* and *Keeton*, the programs were able to show the court that they had consistent requirements that students adhere to the counseling code of ethics, that their remediation processes were academic exercises rather than disciplinary actions, and that they had an unwavering commitment to the separation of personal religious and ethical principles from the professional requirements of counseling clients. Supporting language was included in student

---

[1]Both Ward and Keeton were represented by the Alliance Defense Fund which, according to its Web site, is "a legal alliance of Christian attorneys and like-minded organizations defending the right of people to freely live out their faith." According to the organization's Web site, an appeal is planned in the *Ward* case. www.americansfortruth.com/news/adf-to-appeal-julea-ward-ruling.html.

handbooks and program policies, and the faculty members took care not to insist on a change or suppression of religious beliefs, but only to require adherence to the profession's ethical code. All these factors contributed substantially to the institutions' victories in both cases.

Ward and *Keeton* may also be viewed from the perspective of student academic freedom. For these aspects of the cases, see Section 5.3 of this *Supplement*.

* * * *

On occasion an institution will deny a degree to a student who has completed all academic requirements satisfactorily, but who commits a crime or serious disciplinary infraction and is denied a degree on that basis (see, for example, *Harwood v. Johns Hopkins Univ., SA 2d*, pp. 249–50). In *Rosenthal v. New York University*, 2010 U.S. Dist. LEXIS 95080 (S.D.N.Y. 11/13/10), Rosenthal had completed all of his course work for the MBA degree from NYU. Unbeknownst to the business school faculty and dean, Rosenthal, who worked for Pricewaterhouse Coopers, had committed securities fraud by providing "insider information" about a publicly traded company to his brother. Rosenthal did not advise NYU that he was under investigation for securities fraud, or that he pleaded guilty to conspiracy to commit securities fraud. NYU learned of Rosenthal's guilty plea and charged him with a violation of the student code of conduct. A hearing was held (after Rosenthal was released from prison), and the business school's Judiciary Committee found that he had violated both the school's honor code and its code of conduct and recommended that he not be awarded the degree. The faculty concurred, and Rosenthal sued for breach of contract and a declaration that the degree had been awarded.

The court reviewed all of the steps taken by NYU to consider whether Rosenthal should be awarded the degree and found that the school had complied with its policies, that the process followed was fair to the plaintiff, and that the faculty had the authority to decide whether or not to award degrees. NYU, said the court, had no contractual obligation to award Rosenthal the MBA degree.

Sec. 8.3. *Sexual Harassment of Students by Faculty Members*

Another sexual harassment case brought under Section 1983, *Cox v. Sugg*, 484 F.3d 1062 (8th Cir. 2007), reached a result similar to *Hayut* (*SA 2d*, pp. 418–19) but provided a new twist in the court's reasoning. The student-plaintiff had sued a professor (the alleged harasser), the university president, and the university chancellor individually; Title IX therefore could not apply (see *SA 2d*, p. 737), and the case proceeded as a Section 1983 suit asserting a violation of the equal protection clause. The court was concerned, however, about construing Section 1983 so broadly that it "would trump the Supreme Court's careful crafting of the implied statutory damage action under Title IX." To avoid such a result, the court applied the Title IX liability standards for institutions (see *SA*

2d, p. 417) to the equal protection claims against the president and chancellor as individuals. Finding that the student had not presented sufficient proof that the president or chancellor had actual notice or was deliberately indifferent, the court determined that these defendants were entitled to qualified immunity under Section 1983 (see *SA 2d*, Sec. 4.4.4) and dismissed the case against them. Regarding the professor, however, the court determined that the Section 1983 claims "pending against [him] in the district court are analytically distinct" and therefore could still be heard by the district court.

In a later sexual harassment case presenting similar issues, *Fitzgerald v. Barnstable School Committee*, 129 S.Ct. 788 (2009) (see Sec. 14.9.3 of this *Supplement*), the U.S. Supreme Court did not express concern, as did the court in *Cox*, that Section 1983 claims could "trump" Title IX implied causes of action; and, unlike *Cox*, the Court in *Barnstable* did not suggest that Title IX standards of liability would apply as such to Section 1983 suits. Rather, the Court acknowledged that the protections under the two sources of law "diverge" in various ways and that "the standards for establishing liability may not be wholly congruent."

* * * *

The case of *Godfrey v. Princeton Theological Seminary*, 952 A.2d 1034 (N.J. 2008) provides another example of how a student harassment victim may bring a claim under a state nondiscrimination law. The case, which is discussed in Section 7.1 of this *Supplement*, also illustrates that students could bring claims involving alleged harassers who are neither other students nor faculty members.

Sec. 8.4. *Evaluating Students with Disabilities*

8.4.1. *Overview.* The amendments to the ADA (see Sec. 4.5.2.5. of this *Supplement*) may result in greater success for students who seek accommodations from testing organizations. In particular, the expanded list of "major life activities," which now includes reading, may enable students with learning disorders or other disabilities that affect their reading speed to make successful accommodation claims. For example, in *Jenkins v. National Board of Medical Examiners*, 2009 U.S. App. LEXIS 2660 (6th Cir. 2/11/09) (unpublished), a federal appellate court reversed the trial court's award of summary judgment to the National Board of Medical Examiners (NBME). That court had followed the U.S. Supreme Court's rulings in the *Sutton* trilogy that had required courts to consider mitigating measures in determining whether or not an individual had a disability that met the law's definition. Those cases are no longer binding because of the amendment of the ADA. In *Jenkins*, the trial court had determined that the plaintiff was not disabled. The appellate court made no findings with respect to the merits, but remanded the case to the trial court to reconsider the plaintiff's claims in light of the new definition of "disability" contained in the amended ADA.

8.4.4. Requests for programmatic or instructional accommodations.

A law student with learning disabilities who claimed that the accommodations provided to her were inadequate has survived the law school's motion to dismiss. In *Di Lella v. University of District of Columbia David A. Clarke School of Law*, 2008 U.S Dist. LEXIS 59143 (D.D.C. August 5, 2008), the student had been promised a variety of academic accommodations, including permission to tape classroom lectures. The law school had apparently agreed to transcribe the tapes for the student. The student alleged that the transcripts were provided late, or not provided at all, and required her to reschedule examinations and disadvantaged her in other ways. She also alleged that the law school retaliated against her for complaining about a professor's public disclosure to the class that the plaintiff had learning disabilities by reporting her alleged plagiarism to the Academic Standards Committee. She also claimed a Section 1983 denial of due process, asserting that the hearing conducted by the committee was defective.

The trial court rejected the law school's motion to dismiss the failure to accommodate and retaliation claims. With respect to the due process claim, however, the court ruled that the plaintiff had received sufficient notice of the charges against her and had had an opportunity to respond to them. The court dismissed her Section 1983 claim.

Although the case was not decided on the merits, the trial court's refusal to dismiss the student's failure to accommodate claim is unusual, given that most students are unsuccessful when they challenge the sufficiency of the academic accommodations they had been given. The difference in this case appears to be that the student claimed that several accommodations she had been promised were not provided, rather than that the accommodations that the school agreed to provide, and did provide, were inadequate.

* * * *

A federal appellate court has clarified the right of a graduate student who is an employee as well as a student to pursue an ADA claim under Title III of the law, which does not require exhaustion of administrative remedies, as do claims brought under Title I (which addresses employment). In *McInerney v. Rensselaer Polytechnic Inst.*, 505 F.3d 135 (2d Cir. 2007), a research assistant with several neurological disorders was admitted to a doctoral program in engineering but failed his doctoral candidacy examination because, he alleged, he did not receive the accommodations he had requested. The trial court dismissed all of the plaintiff's ADA claims because he failed to exhaust his administrative remedies with the Equal Employment Opportunity Commission, as required by Title I of the ADA. But Title III, under which the plaintiff had sued, does not require administrative exhaustion, according to the appellate court. (Title III requires places of "public accommodation," including private colleges and universities, to accommodate qualified individuals with disabilities. See *SA 2d*, pp. 703–5.) The plaintiff had dual status as an employee and a student, and the appellate court vacated the ruling of the trial court, stating that the plaintiff's Title III claims must be tried.

On remand, the trial court rejected the university's motion for summary judgment on all of the plaintiff's ADA complaints, stating that material facts were in dispute and the case must be tried. 669 F. Supp. 2d 117 (N.D.N.Y. 2010).

9

The Disciplinary Process

Sec. 9.1. *Disciplinary and Grievance Systems*

9.1.3. Codes of student conduct. A federal trial court has rejected a student's claim that the student code of conduct at Southern Oregon University is unconstitutionally overbroad and vague and violated his free speech rights. In *Harrell v. Southern Oregon University*, 2009 U.S. Dist. LEXIS 101342 (D. Ore. 10/30/09), a student sought a preliminary injunction to halt discipline meted out for violating the university's code of student conduct. Harrell was charged with being disruptive and intimidating in an online course, a violation of the university's requirement that students not "display[]defiance or disrespect of others." Although the trial court acknowledged that these words could be clearer, it noted that university officials had warned Harrell against the *ad hominem* attacks and belittling behavior in which he had engaged. The court noted that a college classroom is not a public forum "where each student has an absolute constitutional right to say whatever he pleases, when he pleases, however he pleases, for as long and as often as he pleases. This is not talk radio." A federal appellate court affirmed the trial court's ruling. 381 Fed. Appx. 731 (9th Cir. 2010).

9.1.4. Judicial systems. A federal appellate court has affirmed a case in which a trial court ruled that denying students facing both a campus disciplinary hearing and state criminal charges the right to counsel violated their due process rights. In *Holmes v. Poskanzer*, 2008 U.S. Dist. LEXIS 13545 (N.D.N.Y. 2/21/08), *affirmed*, 342 Fed. Appx. 651 (2d Cir. 2009), two students who were disciplined for harassing a university administrator claimed that the discipline violated their due process rights and was in retaliation for their criticism of university administration. The trial court ruled that, although the denial of counsel violated due process because the students were facing criminal charges for the same behavior, that right was not clearly established in the Second Circuit when the situation arose, and thus the defendants were protected by qualified immunity. A student's right to counsel at a campus hearing when the student also faces a criminal hearing for the same conduct is now established in the Second Circuit as well as in the First Circuit (*Gabrilowitz v. Newman*, 582 F.2d 100 (1st Cir. 1978)).

Sec. 9.2. Disciplinary Rules and Regulations

9.2.2. Public institutions. Some state colleges and universities are subject to state statutes that regulate the type of due process to which students are entitled if the institution decides to discipline or dismiss the student. *Morris v. Florida Agricultural and Mechanical University*, 23 So.3d 167 (Fla. Dist. Ct. App. 2009) is a good example of such a situation. In *Morris*, a student had been admitted to law school at Florida A&M University. Although it was later discovered that there was no official record of his admission, the law school accepted the student's tuition and enrolled him in classes, where he made adequate grades his first semester. The law school later learned that a staff member in the admissions office had "fabricated" admission and registration records for Morris. The law school then dismissed Morris without a hearing and without giving Morris an opportunity to review the records relevant to his dismissal or to question the staff members who allegedly fabricated his admissions and registration information. Morris sued, and the court ruled that the school was required to give Morris a hearing prior to his dismissal. Florida's Administrative Procedure Act, Fla. Stat. §120.68(1) (2008), provides that if a state agency takes a final action that adversely affects an individual without holding a hearing, and the validity of the agency's action depends on disputed facts, the district court must reverse the agency action. Because no hearing was held prior to the dismissal, the court ruled that the law school must afford Morris a hearing.

* * * *

A decision of a state appellate court reminds administrators of the importance of following the institution's policies and procedures, particularly when claims of due process violations are made. In *Alpha Eta Chapter of Pi Kappa Alpha Fraternity v. University of Florida*, 982 So. 2d 55 (Fla. App. 1 Dist. 2008), the university suspended the fraternity, after holding a hearing, on the grounds of alleged violations of the university's alcoholic beverage policy. The university relied on hearsay testimony of witnesses by police officers who had interviewed them or by submitting videotapes to the disciplinary hearing panel rather than producing those witnesses at the hearing. According to the university's rules, individuals or organizations charged with violations of university policy "shall be accorded the right to . . . [q]uestion adverse witnesses." The court sided with the fraternity and affirmed the ruling of the trial court that "denial by a public university of a right accorded by its own conduct code to question adverse witnesses requires reversal [of the university's decision] in a case such as this." Without the hearsay evidence, said the court, there was insufficient evidence to support the findings of the disciplinary board; the court ordered the university to reinstate the fraternity.

9.2.4. Disciplining students with psychiatric illnesses.

College decision makers face difficult issues when a student with a psychiatric disorder claims that his or her misconduct was attributable to the effects of the disorder. In *Bhatt v. University of Vermont*, 958 A.2d 637 (Vt. 2008), the university dismissed a medical student after it determined that he had falsified evaluations for several clinical rotations, as well as falsely claiming that he had graduated from his undergraduate institution *magna cum laude*. The student stated that he had Tourette's Syndrome and obsessive-compulsive disorder, and that the misconduct was related to these disabilities. He argued that dismissal was too severe a sanction, given the nature of his disabilities. After convening two hearings, the disciplinary committee dismissed him because of his "deception, dishonesty, and perpetration of fraud." When the medical school rejected the former student's application for readmission, the student sued under the state's law forbidding discrimination by a public accommodation (9 V.S.A. §§4500–4507).

The court characterized the dismissal decision as having been made on "academic and ethical" grounds, and thus entitled to deference by the court. The court also noted that the former student had not sought an accommodation until after he had engaged in the misconduct, and then only to mitigate his punishment. Saying that the purpose of disability discrimination laws was not to give individuals who engage in misconduct a "second chance," the court affirmed the trial court's award of summary judgment to the university.

Sec. 9.3. Procedures for Suspension, Dismissal, and Other Sanctions

9.3.2. Public institutions: Disciplinary sanctions

9.3.2.3. Hearing.

A federal trial court decision provides a good reminder of the importance of giving students who are disciplined for misconduct a meaningful hearing, as well as the importance of dealing with behavior problems promptly in order to avoid retaliation claims. In *Castle v. Marquardt*, 632 F. Supp. 2d 1317 (N.D. Ga. 2009), a nursing student was suspended for egregious misconduct, including threatening fellow students with physical harm and regularly disrupting classes. Just prior to her suspension, the student had informed administrators that one of her instructors was dismissing class after only an hour when the class was scheduled to run for several hours. The instructor was dismissed immediately, and the student was suspended for misconduct. The student claimed a violation of procedural due process and retaliation because she had complained about the behavior of the instructor.

Although the college argued that it had given the student a hearing prior to her dismissal, the court found that the "hearing" had actually been a meeting at which the college's decision to suspend her was presented to her, and that she had not been interviewed as part of the college's investigation into the complaints about her. For that reason, the court determined that summary judgment for the college on the plaintiff's procedural due process claim was inappropriate. Similarly, the court ruled that the two-day period between the plaintiff's reporting of her instructor's misconduct, during which time college administrators interviewed a number of students and faculty but not the plaintiff, would allow a jury to conclude that the suspension was retaliatory, and thus summary judgment for the college was inappropriate.

9.3.3. Public institutions: The legal distinction between disciplinary sanctions and academic sanctions.
Graduate programs in certain disciplines may require students not only to comply with the ethical codes of the discipline or profession but also to agree to the program's nondiscrimination policies. In *Ward v. Wilbanks*, discussed in Sections 5.3 and 8.2 of this *Supplement*, a student enrolled in the graduate program in counseling was dismissed for "unethical" and "unprofessional" conduct. The student, whose religious beliefs do not allow her to condone or enable homosexual activity, had asked to reassign a client in a counseling practicum to another student because the client was seeking advice about his homosexual relationship. She was dismissed from the program when she refused to comply with the counseling code of ethics. The court characterized the requirement that students comply with the ethics code as an academic requirement rather than a conduct requirement, and used a deferential standard of review in determining that the university had not violated the student's constitutional rights.

* * * *

A federal appellate court has affirmed the ruling of a trial court that a graduate student dismissed from a public university has no property right in continued enrollment. In *Davis v. George Mason University*, 395 F. Supp. 2d 331 (E.D. Va. 2005), *affirmed*, 193 Fed. Appx. 248 (4th Cir. 2006), the student had received two failing grades in required courses during his first year in the program. He requested a retroactive withdrawal from the second course, which was denied. In rejecting the student's due process claim, the trial court ruled that neither state statute nor case law created a property right in enrollment in a public university. Even assuming that such a right existed, said the court, Davis was on notice of the graduate program's policy on withdrawals, and his circumstances did not comply with the limited opportunity for withdrawals, which defeated his procedural and substantive due process claims. And because the graduate program's student handbook specifically stated that the handbook was not a contract, the student's breach of contract claim failed as well.

Selected Annotated Bibliography

Sec. 9.3. (Procedures for Suspension, Dismissal, and Other Sanctions)

Geller, Randolph. *Criminal Conduct of Students: The Institution's Response* (Nat'l Ass'n of College & Univ. Attys., 2007) (monograph). Focuses on criminal conduct and admissions, financial aid, and housing; the circumstances under which an institution may discipline a student for conduct that is criminal in nature, including a discussion of due process and the postponement of disciplinary proceedings when criminal charges are likely or pending; criminal conduct and the awarding of degrees; and the impact of various laws and regulations, including FERPA, on criminal conduct by students.

10

Students' Freedom of Expression

Sec. 10.1. Student Protests and Freedom of Speech

10.1.1. Student free speech in general. *Hagel v. Portland State University*, 203 P.3d 226 (Or. Ct. App. 2009), provides an example of how student free expression may be protected by state constitutions. The university had expelled a student for making statements that he wanted to harm or kill a staff member and his family. The student challenged his expulsion as violating Article 1, Section 8 of the Oregon Constitution, the free speech clause. Although the Oregon Court of Appeals rejected the student's challenge, its discussion of Article I, Section 8 made clear that, in other types of circumstances, the provision would be a source of substantial protection for student free speech (see 203 P.3d at 229).

10.1.3. Regulation of student protest

Clarification. "Heckler's veto" problems (*SA 2d*, pp. 487–88) may arise not only when protesters are being heckled or otherwise disrupted by onlookers, but also when a single speaker or panel of speakers (who may not be protesting anything) is disrupted by members of the audience—who in effect become the protesters. An invited outsider may deliver a speech on campus, for example, and students in the audience may seek to protest against the speaker's message or against a position that the speaker had previously taken on a public issue. To accomplish their objective, the students may use such tactics as calling out, questioning, chanting, booing, or rhythmic clapping. A recent case, *State of Vermont v. Colby*, 972 A.2d 197 (Vt. 2009), suggests that such situations may implicate the same free speech principles, and much the same analysis, as the situations where onlookers heckle protesters.

Audience members' rights to interrupt a speaker depend in the first instance on whether, in context, their actions would be considered expressive activities within the ambit of the free speech clause. If they are, as they usually would be in the type of situation described above, then the extent to which these activities are protected, according to the *Colby* case and an earlier California case that it relies on (*In re Kay*, 464 P.2d 142 (Cal. 1970)), depends on whether the activity "substantially impairs the effective conduct" of the meeting or the effective delivery of the speech. Since this is a First Amendment test, it is applicable in the first instance only to situations arising at public institutions. But the test (and the First Amendment) could also apply to situations arising in private institutions if (1) their administrators call in local police to handle the situation, or (2) the protesting audience members are subsequently charged under a state statute prohibiting disorderly conduct or other pertinent misconduct. The *Colby* case illustrates this circumstance, since it involves the validity of a disorderly conduct conviction of protesting audience members at a commencement ceremony of a private institution.

The "substantial impairment" test apparently parallels the "substantial disruption" test applicable to situations where onlookers heckle protesters (see pp. 486–87). The impairment test requires an objective assessment of "the severity of the disruption" based on "the actual impact" of the audience members' activity "on the course of the meeting." The "timing, duration, [and] intensity" of the activity must all be considered. The assessment must also include consideration of "the nature and character of [that] particular kind of meeting, . . . the purpose for which it is held, and . . . the usage and practice governing such meetings."[1] The disruption must arise from the protesting audience members' own actions and not merely from the reactions of other audience members or the institution to the protesting audience members' expressive activity. Also pertinent is whether the protesting audience members were asked to cease their activity and whether they complied with the request. Rudeness, statements that offend other audience members, or a very brief interruption of the speech or meeting, without more, are usually not sufficient to constitute a "substantial impairment." Making "numerous and sustained efforts to disrupt a meeting [or speaker] after being asked to desist" usually will be sufficient to constitute "substantial disruption." (The quotes in this paragraph come from the *Colby* case and from *In re Kay* and other cases quoted in *Colby*.)

As is evident from the discussion above, the First Amendment rights of three groups are intertwined in these heckler's veto situations: the rights of the speaker to speak and be heard; the rights of objecting audience members to protest; and the other audience members' right to assemble and "right to hear" the speaker. All three sets of rights must be taken into account, and some kind of balance must be struck. As the court in *In re Kay* cautioned: "Freedom of everyone to talk at once can destroy the right of anyone effectively to talk at all. Free expression can expire as tragically in the tumult of license as in the silence of censorship . . ." (464 P.2d at 149).

---

[1]These considerations parallel those that courts may use under the public forum doctrine (*SA 2d*, sec. 10.1.2). Some courts may therefore resort to the public forum doctrine as another source of legal principles that would sometimes be used in the type of situation that is the focus of this discussion.

Sec. 10.2. Speech Codes and the Problem of Hate Speech

10.2.2. The case law on hate speech and speech codes. The case of *College Republicans at San Francisco State University v. Reed*, 523 F. Supp. 2d 1005 (N.D. Cal. 2007), provides another example of the newer, more varied, controversies that have arisen post 9/11 (see *SA 2d*, p. 503). After holding an "Anti-Terrorism" rally on campus, the College Republicans were charged by the university with violating several California State University system regulations, especially one stating that

> Students are expected to be good citizens and to engage in responsible behaviors that reflect well upon their university, to be *civil* to one another and to others in the campus community, and to contribute positively to student and university life. [Cal. Code Regs., Title 5, §41301(a).]

The student organization claimed that the language requiring students to be "civil" would prevent them from engaging in many expressive activities and therefore was unconstitutionally overbroad. In granting the organization's motion for a preliminary injunction, the court held there was a strong likelihood that the organization would prevail on this claim, in particular because

> the requirement "to be civil to one another" and the directive to eschew behaviors that are not consistent with "good citizenship" reasonably can be understood as prohibiting the kind of communication that it is necessary to use to convey the full emotional power with which a speaker embraces her ideas or the intensity and richness of the feelings that attach her to her cause. Similarly, mandating civility could deprive speakers of the tools they most need to connect emotionally with their audience, to move their audience to share their passion. [523 F. Supp. 2d at 1019.]

* * * *

The *College Republicans* case, immediately above, also provides a vivid illustration of "the 'emotive content' principle," the second free speech principle set out on *SA 2d*, p. 504. As the above discussion of the case indicates, the court investigated whether the enforcement of the university's civility requirement would be at odds with the emotional content principle. In concluding that the requirement likely would be at odds, the court gave this helpful explanation of the principle:

> There also is an emotional dimension to the effectiveness of communication. Speakers, especially speakers on significant or controversial issues, often want their audience to understand how passionately they feel about their subject or message. For many speakers on religious or political subjects, for example, having their audience perceive and understand their passion, their intensity of feeling, can be the single most important aspect of an expressive act. And for many people, what matters most about a particular instance of communication is whether it inspires emotions in the audience, i.e., whether it has the

emotional power to move the audience to action or to a different level of interest in or commitment to an idea or cause. For such people, the effectiveness of communication is measured by its emotional impact, by the intensity of the resonance it creates. [523 F. Supp. 2d at 1018–19.][2]

10.2.3. Guidelines for dealing with hate speech on campus. The fourth potential approach to regulating hate speech—the infringement of privacy or "captive audience" approach (*SA 2d*, pp. 507–8)—is extensively analyzed in Melissa Weberman, "University Hate Speech Policies and the Captive Audience Doctrine," 36 *Ohio Northern U.L. Rev.* 553 (2010).

---

[2] If the emotive content were to move the audience to *violent* action, the incitement doctrine would become involved. See *Brandenburg v. Ohio*, 395 U.S. 444 (1969); and see also *SA 2d*, pp. 488 and 515.

11

Student Organizations and Their Members

Sec. 11.1. Student Organizations

11.1.4. *Principle of nondiscrimination.* The U.S. Supreme Court has now spoken on the weighty and complex issues arising from public higher educational institutions' application of their nondiscrimination policies to student organizations that claim a constitutional right to exclude certain students from membership or office holding. By a 5 to 4 vote in *Christian Legal Society v. Martinez,* 130 S. Ct. 2971 (2010), the Court affirmed the decision of the U.S. Court of Appeals for the Ninth Circuit in *Christian Legal Society Chapter of University of California, Hastings College of the Law v. Kane,* 319 Fed. Appx. 645 (9th Cir. 2009), thus upholding Hastings' application of its nondiscrimination policy to registered student organizations. *Martinez* now replaces *Christian Legal Society v. Walker,* 453 F.3d 853 (7th Cir. 2006) (*SA 2d,* pp. 529–30) as the primary authority on these contentious issues.

At Hastings, registered student organizations (RSOs) receive various benefits, including "financial assistance" from mandatory student activity fee funds, use of law school "channels to communicate with students," use of law school "facilities for meetings and office space," and use of the Hastings "name and logo." In return, RSOs must comply with pertinent school policies, including the nondiscrimination policy stating that: "Hastings College of Law shall not discriminate unlawfully on the basis of race, color, religion, national origin, ancestry, disability, age, sex, or sexual orientation." The local chapter of the Christian Legal Society (CLS) had applied for and was denied the status of an RSO because it did not comply with this policy. The chapter asserted that the national organization of the CLS requires its chapters to use a set of bylaws that includes a Statement of Faith to be signed by any student seeking to become a member or officer of the chapter. Hastings claimed that this Statement of Faith was not in compliance with the religion and sexual orientation provisions of Hastings' nondiscrimination policy. To become recognized, Hastings advised, the CLS chapter would have to open its membership to all students regardless of their religious beliefs or sexual orientation. The chapter declined to do so.

CLS brought suit, asserting that Hastings had violated its rights to free speech, freedom of expressive association, and free exercise of religion under the First Amendment. The parties agreed on a joint stipulation of facts that became important throughout the litigation. In an unpublished opinion, the federal district court rejected the chapter's claims and granted summary judgment in favor of Hastings. On appeal, the Ninth Circuit affirmed the decision of the district court but not its reasoning. In a one-paragraph opinion, the appellate court reasoned: "The parties stipulate that Hastings imposes an open membership rule on all student groups—all groups must accept all comers as voting members even if those individuals disagree with the mission of the group. The conditions on recognition are therefore viewpoint neutral and reasonable" (citing *Truth v. Kent School Dist.*, 542 F.3d 634, 649–50 (9th Cir. 2008)). Cryptic though it is, the appellate court's statement, read along with the cited pages from *Truth*, apparently accepts that the Hastings nondiscrimination policy restricted the CLS chapter's speech, not just its conduct; that free speech analysis of the restriction is therefore appropriate; that the requirements applicable to a limited public forum (see *SA 2d*, Sec. 10.1.2) apply to the case; and that the nondiscrimination policy, being "viewpoint neutral" and "reasonable," complies with the requirements for restricting access to a limited public forum.

In affirming the Ninth Circuit, the Supreme Court took a similar approach to the case, emphasizing limited public forum analysis and relying on the parties' joint stipulation of facts. To understand the Court's opinion and its limits, it is critical to see exactly how the Court framed the issue. As stated by Justice Ginsburg, who wrote the majority opinion:

> This case concerns a novel question regarding student activities at public universities: May a public law school condition its official recognition of a student group—and the attendant use of school funds and facilities—on the organizations' agreement to open eligibility for membership and leadership to all students? [130 S. Ct. at 2978.]

According to the facts stipulated by the parties, "Hastings requires that registered student organizations allow *any* student to participate, become a member, or seek leadership positions in the organization, regardless of [her] status or beliefs." This requirement was called an "all-comers" policy. Sticking to this stipulation, the Court majority "consider(ed) only whether conditioning access to a student-organization forum on compliance with an all-comers policy violates the Constitution." The issue addressed and answered by the Court, therefore, was both more limited and more general than it might have been. The Court did not resolve the constitutionality of the Hastings RSO policy "on its face," since it framed the issue in terms of the stipulation of facts rather than doing its own line by line review of Hastings' written nondiscrimination policy or related RSO policies (as CLS and the Court's four dissenters had urged it to do). Nor did the Court resolve the constitutionality of the Hastings RSO policy "as applied" particularly to CLS or to religious student organizations, since it was constrained by the joint stipulation and thus explored neither the range of potential facts concerning the policy's application to CLS (or other religious organizations) or the policy's specific impact on CLS. Thus, while the Court answered a highly important core question regarding the clash between free expression and nondiscrimination, at the same time it left for another day various other constitutional questions concerning the particular nondiscrimination policies of particular institutions and how they actually work in practice and as applied to particular student groups.

Equally important as the Court's framing of the issue is its framing of the analysis. The Court focused primarily on CLS's free speech challenge, using public forum principles (see *SA 2d*, Sec. 10.1.2) to reject the challenge. "Our decisions make clear, and the parties agree, that Hastings, through its RSO program, established a *limited* public forum" (citing *Rosenberger v. Rector and Visitors of Univ. of Virginia*, 515 U.S. 819, 829 (1995); emphasis added). "[W]e are persuaded that our limited-public-forum precedents adequately respect . . . CLS's speech . . . rights, and fairly balance those rights against Hastings' interests as property owner and education institution."

The two requirements for validly excluding a particular class of speakers or topics from a limited public forum are that the exclusion be: (a) "viewpoint neutral" and (b) "reasonable" in light of the forum's purposes (see *Rosenberger*, 515 U.S. at 829–30; *SA 2d*, Sec. 10.1.2, pp. 482–83). The Court in *Martinez* held that the Hastings "all-comers" policy (as described in the parties' fact stipulation) met both requirements.[1]

Regarding the first requirement, the Court emphasized the neutral, nondiscriminatory character of the all-comers policy. According to the majority:

> It is . . . hard to imagine a more viewpoint-neutral policy than one requiring *all* student groups to accept *all* comers . . . . Hastings' all-comers requirement draws no distinction between groups based on their message or perspective. An all-comers condition on access to RSO status, in short, is textbook viewpoint neutral. [130 S. Ct. at 2993.]

In applying the second requirement, reasonableness, the majority focused on Hastings' statement of the purposes of the all-comers policy and on Hastings'

---

[1] The Court extracted these two requirements for a limited public forum predominantly from the U.S. Supreme Court's decision in *Rosenberger v. Rector & Visitors of Univ. of Virginia*, 515 U.S. 819 (1995) (see *Martinez* at 2984–86, 2988; see also *SA 2d*, Sec. 11.1.5, pp. 534–36). In *Rosenberger*, the Court explained that these requirements apply to the exclusion of particular classes of speakers or topics from a limited public forum (515 U.S. at 829–30). This is the type of issue raised in *Martinez*. Were the issue one of restricting the speech of a speaker or class of speakers that already had access to the limited public forum, a different set of requirements would apply— strict scrutiny requirements akin to those for a traditional public forum (see *SA 2d*, Sec. 10.1.2). In the earlier case of *Christian Legal Society v. Walker* (above), there was confusion over which type of question was involved and which set of requirements therefore applied (*Walker*, 453 F.3d at 865–67). In suggesting that strict scrutiny may be applicable, the *Walker* majority may have mixed up the two sets of requirements for a limited public forum; or it may have assumed that, since CLS had been admitted to the forum and later was rejected, the latter set of requirements applied (the strict scrutiny requirements) rather than the former (the requirements applied in *Martinez*).

educational policy judgments that supported the all-comers concept. Prefacing its determination on reasonableness, the majority made clear that it would accord a measure of deference to Hastings' policy judgments (see *SA 2d*, sec. 2.2.3) because "judges lack the on-the-ground expertise and experience of school administrators," and courts should therefore "resist 'substitut[ing] their own notions of sound educational policy for those of the school authorities which they review'" (130 S. Ct. at 2988, quoting *Board of Education of Hendrick Hudson Central School District v. Rowley*, 458 U.S. at 206 (1982)). Reviewing the parties' arguments about reasonableness from this perspective, the majority concluded, *inter alia*, that Hastings "may decide, reasonably in our view, 'that the . . . educational experience is best promoted when all participants in the [student-organization] forum must provide equal access to all students'" (130 S. Ct. at 2989, quoting Brief for Hastings), and that Hastings "reasonably adheres to the view that an all-comers policy, to the extent it brings together individuals with diverse backgrounds and beliefs, 'encourages tolerance, cooperation, and learning among students'" (130 S. Ct. at 2990, quoting from the Appendix in the record on appeal).

CLS's second challenge to the Hastings policy—the freedom of expressive association challenge (see generally *SA 2d*, Sec. 11.1.1, p. 513)—was concisely dispatched by the Court. CLS had urged the Court to analyze this claim under a different line of cases using a somewhat stricter standard of review than the limited public forum cases. Declining the invitation, the Court determined that its public forum analysis "suppl[ies] the appropriate framework for assessing . . . CLS's . . . expressive-association claims" as well. The Court reasoned that:

> First, . . . speech and expressive-association rights are closely linked. . . . When these intertwined rights arise in exactly the same context, it would be anomalous for a restriction on speech to survive constitutional review under our limited-public-forum . . . test only to be invalidated as an impermissible infringement of expressive association.
>
> Second, and closely related, the strict scrutiny we have applied in some settings to laws that burden expressive association would, in practical effect, invalidate a defining characteristic of limited public forums—the State may "reserve[e] [them] for certain groups." *Rosenberger*, 515 U.S. at 829. . . .
>
> The same ground rules must govern both speech and association challenges in the limited-public-forum context, lest strict scrutiny trump a public university's ability to "confin[e] a [speech] forum to the limited and legitimate purposes for which it was created." *Rosenberger*, 515 U.S. at 829 . . . .
>
> Third, this case fits comfortably within the limited-public-forum category, for CLS, in seeking what is effectively a state subsidy, faces only indirect pressure to modify its membership policies; CLS may exclude any person for any reason if it forgoes the benefits of official recognition. The expressive-association precedents on which CLS relies, in contrast, involved regulations that *compelled* a group to include unwanted members, with no choice to opt out. See, *e.g., Boy Scouts of America v. Dale*, 530 U.S. at 648 (regulation "forc[ed] [the Boy Scouts] to accept members it [did] not desire" (internal quotation marks omitted)); *Roberts v. United States Jaycees*, 468 U.S. at 623 ("There can be no clearer example of

an intrusion into the internal structure or affairs of an association than" forced inclusion of unwelcomed participants.).

Application of the less-restrictive limited-public-forum analysis better accounts for the fact that Hastings, through its RSO program, is dangling the carrot of subsidy, not wielding the stick of prohibition. [130 S. Ct. at 2985–86 (footnotes and some citations omitted).]

CLS's third challenge to the all-comers policy—the free exercise of religion challenge—was summarily rejected by the Court. It relied on *Employment Division v. Smith*, 494 U.S. 872 (1990) (see generally *SA 2d*, Sec. 1.6.2, pp. 37–38), a case holding that government regulations that burden religious practice are nevertheless valid if they are "generally applicable" and religiously "neutral." This case "forecloses" CLS's free exercise argument, the Court reasoned, because the Hastings "all-comers" policy, according to the parties' joint stipulation, was neutral toward religion and generally applicable to all recognized student groups.

Having disposed of CLS's three challenges (over a strenuous dissent by four Justices), the majority concluded:

In requiring CLS—in common with all other student organizations—to choose between welcoming all students and forgoing the benefits of official recognition, . . . Hastings did not transgress constitutional limitations. CLS, it bears emphasis, seeks not parity with other organizations, but a preferential exemption from Hastings' policy. The First Amendment shields CLS against state prohibition of the organization's expressive activity, however exclusionary that activity may be. But CLS enjoys no constitutional right to state subvention of its selectivity. [130 S. Ct. at 2978.]

As suggested above, the Court's limited and generalized ruling leaves various avenues open for future litigation. Here is an overview of the most likely constitutional developments to watch for at public institutions:

1. Issues may arise concerning the "facial" constitutionality (see above) of particular institutions' nondiscrimination or student organization policies. Such issues would require an analysis of the particular wording of particular institutions' written policies. It might be argued, for example, that a policy contains exceptions that prevent it from being a true "all-comers" policy, or that a policy's terms are so vague that one cannot determine whether the standards it sets for recognition are viewpoint neutral. The *Martinez* majority does not address the Hastings policy in this way (see above) but the dissent does illustrate how such arguments might arise (see generally 130 S. Ct. at 3016–20).

2. Issues may arise concerning the constitutionality "as applied" (see above) of particular institutions' RSO policies. Such issues would focus not only on the wording of particular policy provisions but also on the actual operation of the policy, as applied to a particular student organization or type of student organization, a particular practice of a student organization, or some

other particular factual circumstance. For example, CLS argued that Hastings "selectively enforces its all-comers policy" (130 S. Ct. at 2995) and that the policy provides a "pretext" for discrimination against religious student groups—an argument concerning the application of Hastings' policy and its actual effect in operation. The *Martinez* majority did not analyze the Hastings policy in this way, since the parties' joint stipulation of facts did not leave room for such an argument, and neither of the lower courts had addressed the argument. (The majority did note, though, that the Ninth Circuit may consider this argument on remand "if, and to the extent, [the issue] is preserved" (130 S. Ct. at 2995).) Justice Kennedy in his concurrence, however, did provide examples of such arguments, in particular an argument based on a showing in a particular case "that the all-comers policy was either designed or used to infiltrate the group" or otherwise to "stifle [the group's] speech or make it ineffective" (130 S. Ct. at 3000). The dissenters also provided other illustrations of how as-applied challenges might unfold under different sets of facts (see generally 130 S. Ct. at 3016–20).

3. Issues may arise concerning alleged "neutral" restrictions that student organizations impose on membership and office holding. While the Court in *Martinez* held that public institutions may not impose *viewpoint-based* or *viewpoint discriminatory* restrictions on the membership policies of registered student organizations, it also makes clear that "RSOs . . ., in harmony with the all-comers policy, may condition eligibility for membership and leadership on attendance, the payment of dues, and other *neutral* requirements designed to ensure that students join because of their commitment to a group's vitality, not its demise" (130 S. Ct. at 2992 (emphasis added)). In the wake of *Martinez*, there may be challenges to such restrictions as imposed by particular student organizations, challenges to institutional policies that permit such restrictions, or challenges to institutional policies that prohibit RSOs from imposing such restrictions. The key issue often would be whether the restriction or policy in question, on its face or as applied, is genuinely "neutral" rather than viewpoint-based or otherwise discriminatory.

4. Issues may arise concerning institutional RSO policies that include exceptions to the "all-comers" policy—in particular an exception for religious student organizations that allows them to limit membership to adherents to the faith. This question was not before the Court in *Martinez*, and the majority specifically distinguished it:

> The question here . . . is not whether Hastings *could*, consistent with the Constitution, provide religious groups dispensation from the all-comers policy by permitting them to restrict membership to those who share their faith. It is instead whether Hastings *must* grant that exemption. [130 S. Ct. at 2993, n. 24.]

The question left open—whether an institution may provide an exception for student religious groups—could present not only viewpoint-neutrality issues but also establishment clause issues (see generally *SA 2d*, Sec. 1.6.4, and compare *SA 2d*, Sec. 4.7, pp. 190–93) and perhaps equal protection issues as well.

5. Issues may arise concerning the First Amendment rights of discriminatory student organizations that "commonly maintain a presence at universities without official school affiliation" (130 S. Ct. at 2991). Such organizations and their members retain First Amendment free speech rights as well as freedom of association—the right to join together, or associate with one another, to engage in expressive activities (see generally *SA 2d*, Secs. 10.1.1 & 11.1.1). How, then, and to what extent, may institutions regulate these groups, compared to their regulation of recognized student groups? It seems clear from *Martinez* that unrecognized groups, like recognized groups, cannot be subjected to institutional regulations based on the group's or members' viewpoints; in either case, such regulations would constitute unlawful viewpoint discrimination. It also seems clear that institutions, in general, have less regulatory authority over the expressive activities of unrecognized groups that are not subsidized like recognized student groups are, since the institution can use the "carrot of subsidy" (see above) as justification for regulating the latter but not the former. Thus, while *Martinez* permits institutions to impose an all-comers requirement on recognized, subsidized, student groups, it by no means follows that institutions could constitutionally impose the same requirement on unrecognized, unsubsidized groups.

Yet other questions may arise concerning institutional regulation of unrecognized student groups. Such questions may implicate both the extent of the institution's authority to limit the speech or association of unrecognized groups that discriminate, and the extent to which an institution may provide some subsidy (e.g., use of campus meeting rooms and bulletin boards) to unrecognized groups that discriminate without running afoul of federal or state nondiscrimination requirements (see generally 130 S. Ct. at 2991–92).

Student affairs administrators, of course, will not be expected to master all the legal nuances of the issues left open by, or decided by, the Supreme Court in *Martinez*. In-depth involvement of legal counsel is a necessity. An administrator's first step should be to understand fully the concept of the "all-comers" policy as established by the majority in *Martinez*. The next step should be to review (along with counsel) the institution's policies on recognized student groups to determine whether, on their face, they establish a genuine all-comers policy. If so, the administrator should then review the experiences of the institutions' student groups in complying with the all-comers policy, and the experiences of responsible student affairs administrators in implementing and enforcing the all-comers policy. The goal would be to assure that the written all-comers policy remains a genuine all-comers policy in practice, such that the institution will be positioned to defend its policy as constitutional both "on its face" and "as applied."

If the institution's existing policy is not a genuine all-comers policy, the question becomes whether the institution chooses to revise the policy to come into compliance with *Martinez* or, alternatively, whether the institution wants to retain the existing policy. Either way, the administrator should call on counsel to determine whether or how to redraft the policy to come into compliance with *Martinez*.

In addition, administrators will want to keep in mind the distinction between recognized and unrecognized student groups—a distinction affirmed by the Court itself in *Martinez*. As discussed above, institutions may constitutionally impose an all-comers policy on recognized groups, but that is not necessarily the case for unrecognized groups. Moreover, different types of issues may arise concerning the institution's authority over unrecognized groups—for example, issues about permitting or prohibiting use of meeting rooms and other campus facilities by unrecognized student groups that deny certain students membership, leadership, or participation in their activities.

* * * *

Controversies such as those in the *Hastings* case (see above, this *Supplement*) can also arise in private institutions. Since First Amendment claims then would not be available to student organization members, the institution may have more leeway to use its discretion in resolving conflicts. This is especially the case if the institution is a religious institution with its own freedom of religion rights under the First Amendment. In *Romeo v. Seton Hall*, 875 A.2d 1043 (N.J. Super. 2005), for example, the court rejected a gay student's challenge to a Catholic-affiliated university's denial of an application for recognition of a group serving the needs of gay and lesbian students.

The student, on behalf of himself and other students, asserted two claims: (a) that the institution's refusal to recognize the group violated the New Jersey Law Against Discrimination (LAD); and (b) that the institution's denial of recognition was a breach of contract. These are the same two types of claims most likely to be available to students at private institutions in other nonrecognition cases. Regarding the first claim, the court acknowledged that the state LAD did cover sexual orientation and did apply to private sector entities (see, e.g., the *Frank v. Ivy Club* case in *SA 2d*, pp. 528–29). But religious institutions such as Seton Hall, the court held, were exempted from the law.

Regarding the second claim, the court acknowledged that Seton Hall had its own nondiscrimination policy that covered sexual orientation discrimination. But neither the pertinent provisions of this policy nor the student's application for recognition of the group created a contract between the group and the university, particularly "where, as here, the [university] values and mission" that are at issue "address fundamental religious ideals" (875 A.2d at 1050). (For much the same reason, the court also held that the university nondiscrimination policy did not and could not constitute a waiver of the university's exemption from the New Jersey LAD.)

Sec. 11.2. Fraternities and Sororities

11.2.2. Institutional recognition and regulation of fraternal organizations.

When Washington State University revoked recognition of a fraternity on the grounds of illegal drug use and policy violations by its members, the fraternity challenged that decision in state court. In *Alpha*

Kappa Lambda Fraternity v. Washington State University, 216 P.3d 451 (Wash. Ap. Div. 3, 2009), the fraternity challenged the conduct and outcome of the student conduct board, which had found that fraternity members had used illegal drugs and had otherwise violated institutional policy. More specifically, the fraternity asserted that the conduct board's findings were not supported by substantial evidence and that the sanction of five years suspension imposed by the university was arbitrary and capricious.

University policy requires that any recognized student organization comply with university conduct policies. The university had received reports from a local police agency that drug use and drug paraphernalia had been observed at the fraternity house, that the fraternity did not have a resident advisor, as required by university policy, that underage individuals had been served alcohol at fraternity social functions, and that hazing had occurred. The university charged the fraternity and several of its members with violations of the student code of conduct, and a hearing was held. Several police officers testified about drug buys and drug use on fraternity property and by current or former fraternity members and their guests. Several fraternity members were dealing cocaine on fraternity property. The conduct board found the fraternity and its members responsible for all of the policy violations and recommended a five-year suspension, followed by two years of probation. The university followed that recommendation.

The trial court upheld the sanction in all respects, and the appellate court affirmed. The appellate court noted that the university's policies and procedures permitted the admission of hearsay evidence in student conduct hearings, and thus the use of such evidence was not a violation. Nor was the use of evidence based upon confidential sources so unreliable as to be impermissible for the conduct board to consider; furthermore, said the court, there was sufficient evidence beyond that of confidential informants that many members of the fraternity were involved in illegal activities.

With respect to the sanction, the court explained that the conduct board had the discretion to impose a range of sanctions, and it had selected a five-year suspension to ensure that most, if not all, of the current fraternity members would no longer be at the university when the suspension was lifted. The court ruled that the conduct board's action was within its discretion.

* * * *

The Iowa Supreme Court has affirmed a lower court ruling finding that the vice president for student services violated the state's law forbidding the interception of electronic communications in connection with the university's investigation of an alleged hazing incident. In *Iowa Beta Chapter of Phi Delta Theta Fraternity v. State of Iowa, University of Iowa, and Phillip E. Jones*, 763 N.W.2d 250 (Iowa 2009), the university had punished the fraternity for violations of its alcohol policy after a nonmember had submitted a tape recording of a meeting at the fraternity house. The nonmember had hidden a tape recorder in the room used for fraternity meetings, and taped the meeting without the knowledge of those present. The vice president for student services relied on the tape recording to support the sanction against the fraternity. The court ruled that the university, through its vice president, had violated state law because of these actions.

* * * *

A federal appellate court rejected the claims of fraternity members that George Mason University's decision to sanction the fraternity and several of its members violated their First and Fourteenth Amendment rights. In *Iota XI Chapter of Sigma Chi Fraternity v. Patterson et al.*, 566 F.3d 138 (4th Cir. 2009), the university sanctioned the fraternity after five incidents in which other students were sexually assaulted or hazed, and in which chapter members sang and danced in front of the university library. An interim sanction was imposed, which revoked the chapter's recognition, prohibiting it from participating in social events and recruitment. A disciplinary hearing was then held, and the student panel found the fraternity and its members responsible for several of the charges against it. The university revoked the chapter's charter for ten years, forbade its members from forming another fraternity, and published the outcome of the disciplinary hearing in the student newspaper. It also disciplined individual members for later wearing Sigma Chi clothing that identified them as chapter members at George Mason.

The trial court awarded summary judgment to the defendants, and the plaintiffs appealed. With respect to their Fourteenth Amendment due process claim for denial of their right to associate with fellow chapter members, the court ruled that the university had not prohibited the plaintiffs from joining another, different fraternity, but from reconstituting their former chapter of Sigma Chi. Therefore, there was no deprivation of their right to associate with one another. With respect to the chapter's claim that publication of the university's sanctions impaired its property interest in its "good name," the court ruled that the plaintiffs had not identified any injury—"economic or otherwise"—occasioned by the publication of the sanctions. And with respect to the First Amendment claim, the court ruled that the sanctions were sufficiently justified by the misconduct of the chapter and its members, and, even if the members' speech had been abridged as a result of the sanctions, there were other lawful reasons to impose them. The court affirmed the award of summary judgment to the defendants.

Sec. 11.3. The Student Press

11.3.1. General principles. When issues arise concerning regulation of *advertising* in student newspapers at public institutions, the analysis tends to be somewhat different from that for issues concerning regulation of, say, news articles, editorials, or editorial policy. That is because advertising is generally considered to be "commercial speech" that receives a lower level of protection under the First Amendment. In many cases, nevertheless, courts have found the protection to be sufficiently strong to invalidate institutional or state agency regulations of advertising. See, for example, *The Pitt News v.*

Pappert, 379 F.3d 96 (3d Cir. 2004), in which the court held that a state statute regulating alcoholic beverage advertising could not constitutionally be applied to a student newspaper. In a recent case, however, *Educational Media Co. at Virginia Tech v. Swecker,* 602 F.3d 583 (4th Cir. 2010), the court reached the opposite result, upholding a state beverage control board's restriction on alcohol advertising in student newspapers. In this case, student newspapers at Virginia Tech and the University of Virginia challenged a board regulation (3 Va. Admin. Code §5–20–40(B)(3)) that prohibits "various types of advertisements for alcohol in any 'college student publication,' which it defines as any college or university publication that is: (1) prepared, edited, or published primarily by its students; (2) sanctioned as a curricular or extracurricular activity; and (3) 'distributed or intended to be distributed to persons under 21 years of age'" (paraphrasing by the court).

The appellate court acknowledged, as had the *Pitt News* court and other courts, that regulations of commercial speech are to be reviewed under the standards set forth in *Central Hudson Gas & Electric Corp. v. Public Service Commission of New York,* 447 U.S. 557 (1980):

> [1] For commercial speech to come within [the First Amendment], it at least must concern lawful activity and not be misleading. [2] Next, we ask whether the asserted governmental interest is substantial. [3] If both inquiries yield positive answers, we must determine whether the regulation directly advances the government interest asserted, and [4] whether it is not more extensive than is necessary to serve that interest. [447 U.S. at 566; numbering added.]

The parties agreed that the board's regulation met the second part of this four-part test; issues arose, however, under parts 1, 3, and 4.

Regarding the first part of the *Central Hudson* test, the board argued that the advertising at issue concerned *unlawful* activity: drinking of alcoholic beverages by students under age twenty-one. The court rejected this argument since the audience for the advertising was not limited to underage students. Even if the newspapers intended the ads to be primarily for the underage students, the newspapers nevertheless were distributed to many students who were at least twenty-one and therefore could legally drink alcoholic beverages.

For the third part of the test, the court considered whether the regulation "directly advances" the government's interest, which the board asserted to be "combating the serious problem of underage drinking and abusive drinking by college students." The board contended that alcohol ads increase demand for alcohol, and ad bans consequently decrease the demand—a proposition that the board claimed was supported by "history, consensus, and common sense." In particular, the board claimed that, since vendors spend so much money on advertising, it must logically follow that alcohol ads increase demand, thus impinging on the government's interest in limiting underage drinking. The college newspapers responded that the board had not submitted any empirical evidence showing that the alcohol advertising ban decreased demand for alcohol among college students and that the ban is ineffective because college students still see and hear alcohol ads in various other media.

The court sided with the board, agreeing that the relationship between the regulation and the government interest "need not be proven by empirical evidence" but instead "may be supported by 'history, consensus, and simple common sense.'" The court then determined that the board had established the link between advertising and student drinking, in particular because college newspapers play an influential role on campus and because advertisers must have concluded that advertising increases their sales or otherwise they would not invest so much money in it. (The *Pitt News* case reached the opposite conclusion in applying the third part of the *Central Hudson* test.)

Under the fourth part of the test, the government's regulation of commercial speech must be "narrowly drawn" to serve the government's interest. This does not mean that the regulation must be "the least restrictive means possible" for serving the government interest but only that it must have a "reasonable fit" to the government interest. The Board's regulation met this requirement, the court reasoned, because

> [It] is not a complete ban on alcohol advertising in college newspapers. First, it only prohibits certain types of alcohol advertisements. In fact, it allows restaurants to inform readers about the presence and type of alcohol they serve. Second, the restriction only applies to "college student publications"—campus publications targeted at students under twenty-one. It does not, on its face, affect all possible student publications on campus . . . . Further, the Board not only considered non-speech related mechanisms to serve its interest; it actually implemented them through education and enforcement programs. [The Board's regulation] complements these non-speech alternatives. Within the Board's multi-pronged attack on underage and abusive drinking, [the regulation] constitutes an additional prevention mechanism. Without it, either education or enforcement efforts would have to be increased, and given the Board's limited resources, [the regulation] is a cost-effective prevention method that properly complements their non-speech related efforts. [602 F.3d at 591.]

(The court in *Pitt News* also reached the opposite conclusion in applying the fourth prong of the *Central Hudson* test.)

The *Educational Media Co.* case was a 2 to 1 decision. The dissenting judge, relying heavily on *Pitt News*, a case that the majority opinion does not discuss, specifically disagreed with the majority's reasoning under both the third prong and the fourth prong of the *Central Hudson* test. The contrast between the reasoning in the *Educational Media* case and that in the *Pitt News* case, as developed by the dissent in *Educational Media*, is striking. Resolving these differences will be a key to the future development of the law in this area.

12

Athletics

Sec. 12.3. Athletes' Freedom of Speech

Issues regarding student athletes' First Amendment rights may arise not only under the free speech clause but also under the establishment and free exercise clauses. A prime example is the issue of group prayer in the locker room or during a game, implicating both the right to engage in such prayer activities and the right to refrain from participation. For an overview of existing practices and applicable First Amendment law, see Kris Bryant, "Note, Take a Knee: Applying the First Amendment to Locker Room Prayers and Religion in College Sports," 36 *J. of Coll. & Univ. Law* 329 (2009).

Sec. 12.6. Sex Discrimination

A challenge to Title IX's 1979 Policy Interpretation has been rejected by a federal appellate court. In *Equity in Athletics, Inc. v. Department of Education*, 504 F. Supp. 2d 88 (W.D. Va. 2007), *affirmed*, 291 Fed Appx. 517 (4th Cir. 2008), the plaintiff, a not-for-profit nonstock corporation, brought claims under Title IX and the equal protection clause against James Madison University and the U.S. Department of Education. The plaintiffs sought a preliminary injunction to prevent the university from eliminating ten varsity athletic teams in 2007—seven men's teams and three women's teams. The lawsuit also sought a ruling that the Education Department's interpretation of Title IX requirements with respect to the Three Part Test of the 1979 Policy Interpretation violated Title IX because it discriminated against men and denied them equal protection under the U.S. Constitution. The trial court had denied the motion for a preliminary injunction on the grounds that the students were not irreparably harmed—they did not lose their scholarships, and those who wished to continue participating in the eliminated sports had transferred or could transfer to other colleges. That court characterized the greater harm to the university as judicial interference with the university's ability to "chart its own course in providing athletic opportunities" absent a clear showing that it had violated the law. The plaintiffs appealed the denial of the injunction, and the appellate court affirmed.

In the trial on the merits, 675 F. Supp. 2d 660 (W.D. Va. 2009), the trial court granted the defendants' motion to dismiss for failure to state a claim. The court reviewed decisions of other appellate courts with respect to the lawfulness of the Three Prong Test and concluded that reducing athletic opportunities for men violated neither Title IX nor the Equal Protection Clause, saying that Title IX neither required nor prohibited such reductions, and that Title IX's remedial purpose protected the university from equal protection clause liability because it took gender into consideration only in a limited way when making its team reduction decisions. The plaintiff had also claimed that the university's decision—and the 1979 Policy Interpretation—violated the players' associational rights under the First Amendment. The court disposed of that claim briskly, stating that playing on a sports team was neither expressive nor intimate association—the only types of association that courts have recognized as meriting protection under the first amendment. With regard to the plaintiff's contention that the 1979 Policy Interpretation was unreasonable because it examined athletic opportunities in relation to enrollment rather than in relation to expressed interest in participation, the court ruled that the Policy Interpretation was entitled to deference unless the plaintiffs could demonstrate that it was an arbitrary and capricious interpretation of the statute. And with respect to the plaintiff's claims that the university's decision to eliminate the ten sports teams denied those athletes procedural and substantive due process, the court declared that students do not have a property right in participating in intercollegiate athletics, citing *Brennan v. Bd. of Trustees for Univ. of La. Sys.,* 691 So.2d 324, 330 (La. Ct. App. 1997); *Rutledge v. Ariz. Bd. of Regents,* 660 F.2d 1345, 1352 (9th Cir. 1981); *Colo. Seminary v. Nat'l Collegiate Athletic Ass'n,* 570 F.2d 320, 321 (10th Cir. 1978); *Gardner v. Wansart,* 2006 U.S. Dist. LEXIS 69491, at *17 (S.D. N.Y. Sept. 26, 2006); *Lesser v. Neosho Cmty. Coll.,* 741 F. Supp. 854, 861 (D. Kan. 1990); *Hysaw v. Washburn Univ.,* 690 F. Supp. 940, 944 (D. Kansas 1987); and *Nat'l Collegiate Athletic Assoc. v. Yeo,* 171 S.W.3d 863, 870 (Tex. 2005) (see *SA 2d,* pp. 569–70). Without a property right, there could be no procedural or substantive due process violation.

* * * *

A federal appellate court joined another circuit in an interpretation of Title IX with respect to the application of the "actual notice" requirement of *Gebser v. Lago Vista Independent School District* (*SA 2d,* pp. 415–17) to claims brought by plaintiffs with respect to athletic participation opportunities. In *Mansourian v. Regents of the University of California et al.,* 602 F.3d 957(9th Cir. 2010), a federal appellate court ruled that the decision of the University of California at Davis to require women on the varsity wrestling team to beat male wrestlers in their weight class in order to remain on the team violated Title IX because it reduced athletic participation opportunities for women. It also ruled that plaintiffs suing an institution for alleged Title IX violations with respect to the accommodation of the interests of female athletes need not give the institution notice prior to the lawsuit in order to prevail. Contrary to the Supreme Court's requirement of "actual notice" to the institution when a complaint of sexual harassment is made, the court noted that a Title IX complaint about an "affirmative institutional decision" such as a change in policy with respect to a varsity sports team does not require prior notice to the institution. The court explained that "[d]ecisions to create or eliminate teams or to add or decrease roster slots for male or female athletes are official decisions, not practices by individual students or staff. Athletic programs that fail effectively to accommodate students of both sexes thus represent 'official policy of the recipient entity' and so are not covered by *Gebser's* notice requirement." Thus, the court agreed with a similar conclusion reached by the U.S. Court of Appeals for the Fifth Circuit in *Pederson v. Louisiana State University*, 213 F.3d 858 (5th Cir. 2000).

The court also ruled that, when calculating the number of athletics participation opportunities available at an institution, athletes who participate in more than one sport are counted as participants for each sport that they play.

* * * *

The Office of Civil Rights, U.S. Department of Education issued a Policy Clarification on April 20, 2010 that withdraws its 2005 Additional Clarification. The 2005 Clarification had allowed institutions seeking to comply with Title IX through part three of the three-part compliance test to use a student survey to measure student interest in participating in intercollegiate sports (see *SA 2d,* p. 581 for a discussion of the 2005 Policy Clarification). The 2010 Clarification states that OCR does not consider the use of a survey alone sufficient evidence that there is a lack of interest on the part of women students in participation in intercollegiate sports. The "Dear Colleague" letter explaining the Clarification may be viewed at http://ed.gov/about/offices/list/ocr/letters/colleague-20100420.html.

* * * *

A federal appellate court ruled that a student's claim of sexual harassment against her soccer coach could go to trial, vacating a trial court's award of summary judgment to the coach, the university counsel, and the university itself. In *Jennings v. University of North Carolina at Chapel Hill, et al.*, 482 F.3d 686 (4th Cir. 2007) (*en banc*), the full appellate court considered the student's claim. She alleged that the soccer coach, Anson Dorrance, had engaged in sexually charged talk and touching with members of the women's soccer team and had created a hostile environment for her and other team members. She claimed that Dorrance asked the team members about their sexual activity, commented on their body parts, touched some of them inappropriately, and discussed his sexual fantasies, some of which included those students. She also claimed that she reported the alleged harassment to the university counsel, and accused the counsel of not responding appropriately to her complaint.

In determining whether the plaintiff had demonstrated that sexual harassment had occurred such that the university could be found liable, the *en banc* court stated that the plaintiff had to establish four elements:

(1) she was a student at an educational institution receiving federal funds,
(2) she was subjected to harassment based on her sex, (3) the harassment was sufficiently severe or pervasive to create a hostile (or abusive) environment in an educational program or activity, and (4) there is a basis for imputing liability to the institution [482 F.3d at 695].

Because the university received federal funds, the first element was easily met. With respect to the second element, although the university argued that Dorrance's comments were teasing and joking, and were not severe enough to constitute harassment, the court ruled that his comments were "degrading and humiliating to his players because they were women," and constituted sexual harassment. In evaluating whether the plaintiff could meet the third element, the court examined the reasoning of cases involving sexual harassment claims brought under Title VII, and concluded that the frequency of the sexual remarks, Dorrance's power over the plaintiff and other members as their coach, and the age difference between Dorrance (forty-four) and the players (some as young as seventeen) meant that a jury could find that Dorrance's conduct was sufficiently severe and pervasive to create a hostile environment. And the court ruled that the plaintiff's evidence of emotional distress and poor academic achievement were sufficient to allow a jury to conclude that she had been denied access to educational opportunities or benefits.

The court then turned to the fourth element—examining whether there was a basis for imputing liability to the institution. The court used the two-part test created by the U.S. Supreme Court in *Gebser v. Lago Vista Independent School District* (*SA 2d,* pp. 415–17) that an official had actual knowledge of the alleged harassment and that the institution either failed to respond or acted with deliberate indifference to the student's complaint. The court discussed the plaintiff's allegation that she had met with the university counsel, given her examples of Dorrance's behavior and statements, and that the counsel had told her to work it out with Dorrance and had taken no action. The court ruled that this evidence could establish both actual notice to the university and "deliberate indifference" to the allegations.

The court also vacated the summary judgment award for the university on the plaintiff's equal protection claim under Section 1983 (*SA 2d,* Sec. 4.4.4) brought against Dorrance and the university counsel. Claims that the individual defendants were protected by sovereign immunity, said the court, would be addressed at the subsequent trial.

Two judges dissented, stating that they did not believe that the plaintiff could demonstrate that the harassment was severe or pervasive because very few of the sexual remarks were directed at her, and because she had not been deprived of an educational benefit, since she remained a student at the university. They also asserted that the statements about which the plaintiff complained were not made because of her gender (or the gender of her teammates). The dissenters would also have denied the plaintiff's equal protection claim under §1983 because they did not find the harassment to be severe or pervasive.

Selected Annotated Bibliography
Sec. 12.7. (Discrimination on the Basis of Disability)

Lakowski, Terri. "Athletes with Disabilities in School Sports: A Critical Assessment of the State of Sports Opportunities for Students with Disabilities." 27 *Boston University International Law Journal* 283 (2009).

13

Local and State Governments

Sec. 13.1. Local Governments and the Local Community

13.1.2. Community access to the college's campus

13.1.2.2. Exclusion of speakers and events. For additional guidance on drafting legally sound (and policy-wise) regulations, see *Academic Freedom and Outside Speakers* (AAUP 2007), prepared by a subcommittee of Committee A and approved by Committee A as AAUP policy; available at http://www.aaup. org/AAUP/comm/rep/A/outside.htm.

13.1.2.3. Trespass statutes and ordinances, and related campus regulations. An Ohio case provides an example of how probable cause issues may arise in situations where campus or local police are enforcing criminal trespass laws on campus (see *SA 2d*, p. 618). In *Harper v. Amweg*, 2006 WL 745394 (S.D. Ohio, 2006), *affirmed*, 2007 WL 1028803 (6th Cir. 2007), Ohio State University decided to prohibit individuals from selling handmade buckeye necklaces on the university's campus. To implement this decision, the university appointed law enforcement officers and other officials to serve as a "Vendor Detail" that was instructed to order individuals selling the necklaces to leave the campus.

Harper, the plaintiff, was a vendor who had been selling handmade buckeye necklaces on campus. At the start of the 2003 football season, a member of the vendor detail, Officer Amweg, approached Harper while she was selling the necklaces on university property and asked her to leave. Harper asked where she could sell the necklaces and Amweg replied, "Lane Avenue." At the next game, following Amweg's advice, she sold buckeye necklaces in the area of Lane Avenue. Amweg again approached her and asked her to leave the property, stating that his previous advice was mistaken.

As Harper was leaving the property to return to her car, some persons stopped her and asked to buy necklaces. Harper sold them the necklaces and continued on to her car; but before she got there, Amweg and another detail member, Deputy Hamburger, detained her, searched her belongings, and then arrested her. Campus police charged her with criminal trespass under Ohio Revised Code §2911.21, but the charges were later dismissed.

Harper then brought a suit under 42 U.S.C. §1983 against Officer Amweg and Deputy Hamburger, alleging that they had violated her Fourth Amendment rights. Harper claimed that she had been arrested without probable cause, subjected to an illegal search and seizure of her person and belongings, and detained through the use of excessive force.

Regarding probable cause to arrest, the court rejected Harper's claim: "Plaintiff continued to sell buckeye necklaces on Ohio State property despite direct orders not to do so. Based on Plaintiff's disregard for the law, Defendants had probable cause to arrest her for criminal trespass and therefore did not violate Plaintiff's constitutional rights." Similarly, the court rejected Harper's claim that no probable cause existed to search her belongings: "[B]ecause the officers made a lawful arrest, they were justified in conducting a warrantless search of Plaintiff's person and her belongings."

Third, the court considered Harper's claim of excessive force, that is, a claim that the officers had "physically held, moved, and handcuffed her," rejecting this claim as well. It noted that under *Graham v. Connor*, 490 U.S. 386, 396 (1989), "[t]he fourth amendment requires that an officer's use of force be objectively reasonable, and courts must balance the consequences to the individual against the government's interest in effecting the seizure." "In this case, there is no evidence that Plaintiff complained to the officers, nor that she suffered any injury as a result of being handcuffed . . . . The officers were justified in handcuffing Plaintiff as a result of the lawful arrest and to permit them to conduct a lawful search of her person and her belongings."

The district court thus agreed with the defendants and granted summary judgment for Officer Amweg and Deputy Hamburger, concluding that they had not violated Mrs. Harper's Fourth Amendment rights. On appeal, the U.S. Court of Appeals affirmed the decision based on the district court's "well reasoned" opinion. A dissenting judge, although agreeing with most of the majority's opinion, argued that the excessive force claim should be returned to the district court and presented to a jury, since fact questions existed as to the reasonableness of the force used by the arresting officers.

Sec. 13.2. State Government

13.2.5. Open-records laws. A state appellate court has ruled that the National Collegiate Athletic Association (NCAA) is subject to the Florida public records law when a public college or university uses otherwise nonpublic NCAA documents related to allegations of rules violations. In *National Collegiate Athletic Ass'n v. Associated Press*, 18 So. 3d 1201 (Dist. Ct. App. Fla., 1 Dist., 2009), the NCAA had investigated allegations that employees at Florida State University had improperly assisted student athletes. The NCAA had conducted a hearing about the allegations, and had posted a transcript of the hearing, as well as the response of the university's infractions committee, on a secure Web site. The university's attorneys were permitted access to the Web site for the purpose of defending the university against the charges. The court ruled that, although the materials were ordinarily private and not subject to the state's public records laws, the fact that agents of a public university used these materials in the course of "public business" brought them under the ambit of the open public records law, and thus the NCAA was required to disclose the documents.

The NCAA had argued that the records were education records and protected by FERPA (*SA 2d*, Sec. 5.5.1). The court disagreed, noting that student names had been redacted from the documents, and because the students were not identifiable, FERPA did not apply. The NCAA also claimed that the application of the state public records law under these circumstances violated its constitutional rights under the Commerce Clause and the First Amendment. The court rejected both claims. First, the court said, the application of the state's public records law did not burden interstate commerce because had the document involved a Florida entity seeking to avoid public disclosure when it involved a public agency, the outcome of that dispute would have been the same. With respect to the NCAA's claim that the application of the public records law to confidential documents violated its freedom of association rights under *Boy Scouts of America v. Dale* (*SA 2d*, p. 529), the court replied that *Dale* was not relevant to the situation facing the NCAA in that the application of the public records law did not affect the organization's membership policies, but only affected the organization's "ability to conduct [] secret proceedings against a public school in this state" (Id. at 1214).

* * * *

The Supreme Court of Wyoming has interpreted the state's public records law expansively, ruling that a tape recording made secretly by a university employee during a meeting of the university's traffic appeals committee is a public record. In *Sheaffer v. State of Wyoming*, 139 P.3d 468 (Wyoming 2006), the university had argued that the tape was part of a personnel matter, and thus exempt from disclosure, because the manager of transportation services was dismissed based upon the tape. The court disagreed, stating that the tape was a record of official university business because it had been received by a university official, and thus was subject to disclosure.

Sec. 13.2.7. Gun possession laws (new section). Legislative developments concerning guns on campuses have expanded in the wake of various campus shootings, such as occurred at Virginia Tech in 2007, and in the wake of the U.S. Supreme Court's 2008 and 2010 decisions recognizing the right of individuals, under the Second Amendment, to "keep and bear" arms. In *District of Columbia v. Heller*, 128 S. Ct. 2783 (2008), the Court held that the Second Amendment created an individual right that is not limited to arming militias and that various gun control regulations of the District of

Columbia violated this individual right. In *McDonald v. City of Chicago*, 130 S. Ct. 3020 (2010), the Court concluded that the Second Amendment applied not only to the federal government but also to the states, and invalidated city ordinances prohibiting the possession of handguns by private citizens.

There are often two contending, and often incompatible, forces at work in disputes concerning gun control. Viewing events from one perspective, members of a campus community may push for state legislation banning guns from campuses (for community safety). Viewing events from another perspective, other members may push for state legislation permitting guns on campus (for personal protection). Analysis of such legislation, and of campus regulations that may be inconsistent with such legislation, may implicate not only the *Heller* and *McDonald* cases (and the numerous questions about their scope), but may also implicate provisions of the state constitution that (a) grant to particular public universities a range of autonomy from state legislative enactments or (b) establish a state constitutional right to keep and bear arms.

Public institutions in several states have attempted to avoid the application of state legislation that permits students and employees to possess or carry guns on campus if they are licensed. For example, the University of Utah has wrestled with Utah Code §63–98–102, which prohibits state or local entities from promulgating a statute, policy, or rule that in "any way inhibits or restricts the possession or use of firearms on either public or private property." There is no exception for colleges and universities. The university, to the contrary, had had a policy that prohibited faculty, staff, and students from possessing firearms on campus. The state attorney general issued an opinion stating that the university's policy violated state law, and the university then sued the attorney general in state court. The Utah Supreme Court ruled against the university in *University of Utah v. Shurtleff*, 144 P.3d 1109 (Utah 2006). Although the university did enjoy a form of autonomy under the state constitution (see *SA 2d*, Sec. 13.2.2), the court said that constitution also guaranteed the citizens of Utah the right to keep and bear arms. Furthermore, the constitutional autonomy of the university does not limit the legislature's power to exercise "general control and supervision" over the university. Specifically, "the Utah Constitution does not grant the University authority to promulgate firearms policies in contravention of legislative enactments, and it is not our place to do so" (144 P.3d at 1121). And, in response to the university's claim that the firearms law violated its academic freedom, the court responded that, although the university enjoyed "broad powers," it was not free from legislative oversight. The Chief Justice dissented, arguing that the state constitution gave the university the authority to forbid the possession and use of firearms on campus.

Subsequently, in March 2007, the Utah legislature passed S.B. 251, which amends Section 53B-3-103 of the Laws of Utah. The amendment specifically requires the boards of trustees of universities and colleges in Utah to acknowledge "that the Legislature has the authority to regulate, by law, firearms at higher education institutions." After such acknowledgment is made, the law authorizes the board of trustees to allow the colleges and universities under its purview to "make a rule that allows a resident of a dormitory located at the institution to request only roommates who are not licensed to carry a concealed firearm" under the relevant state laws.

In other states, students and student organizations have challenged university regulations or policies that prohibit possession of firearms on campus. In *DiGiacinto v. The Rector and Visitors of George Mason University*, Dkt. #CL-2008–14054 (Fairfax Co. Cir. Ct., Aug. 14, 2009), the plaintiff challenged a regulation promulgated by George Mason University, a public university in Virginia, that prohibits "the possession or carrying of a weapon by any person other than a police officer in academic buildings, administrative office buildings, student/ resident buildings, dining facilities or while attending sporting, entertainment or educational events on the University property." The plaintiff argued that the regulation violated his Second Amendment right to bear arms and that the university did not have the delegated authority to regulate handguns on campus.

The trial court cited *Heller* (see above) but emphasized that the Court's opinion recognized that Second Amendment protections were not absolute, and that prohibitions on guns in "sensitive places such as government buildings and schools" continued to be lawful. The judge thus ruled that George Mason's regulation did not violate the Second Amendment. It then also ruled that the University was not required to seek the legislature's permission in order to ban guns on campus.

In *Students for Concealed Carry on Campus v. Regents of the University of Colorado*, 2010 Colo. App. LEXIS 541, 2010 WL 1492308 (April 15, 2010), a state trial court had rejected a student group's challenge to a University of Colorado prohibition on the possession of "firearms or other weapons" anywhere on a campus of the university by all individuals except certified law enforcement personnel. The group claimed that the regulation violated the state constitution as well as the Colorado Concealed Carry Act. Noting that the regents was a "statewide authority with its own legislative powers over distinct geographical areas" and that state legislation can supplant the authority of the regents "only when a legislative enactment expressly so provides," the trial court ruled that the regents' regulation was an appropriate exercise of the state's police power.

The state appellate court reversed the trial court, ruling that the Colorado law authorizing concealed carrying of handguns did not contain an exemption for colleges and universities. Furthermore, said the court, the students had stated a valid claim that prohibition of concealed weapons on campus violated the state constitution's provision concerning the right to bear firearms for self defense. The court remanded the students' constitutional claim to the trial court for further proceedings. The university appealed that decision to the Colorado Supreme Court, which has agreed to hear the case (2010 Colo. LEXIS 781, 2010 WL 4159242 (Colorado 10/18/10)).

14

The Federal Government

Sec. 14.2. Copyright Law

14.2.2. The fair use doctrine. Despite the clear precedent of *Basic Books v. Kinko's Graphics Corp.* and *Princeton University Press v. Michigan Document Services* (*SA 2d*, p. 677), another copy shop has been found to have violated the copyright law by providing course packs without paying copyright fees. In *Blackwell Publishing, Inc. et al. v. Excel Research Group, LLC*, 661 F.Supp. 2d 786 (E.D. Mich. 2009), the copy shop attempted to skirt copyright infringement liability by having the *student* do the photocopying of the course pack master provided by the copy shop.

The copy shop owner argued that the publisher-plaintiffs had executed contracts with the University of Michigan (whose students used the copy shop) to permit students and professors to make copies of the works for educational use. The defendant argued that he was not selling copyrighted works, but a service—photocopying. The defendant also argued that because the students were doing the copying, and not employees of the copy shop, it was the students who were infringing the copyright, not the copy shop.

The court responded that the "contracts" between the publishers and the university were licensing agreements that permitted students to download and print certain articles, but did not authorize them to do so at a copy shop. Students were the authorized license users, not the copy shop. And because the copy shop made money from the unauthorized copying, which was not permitted by the licensing agreement between the publisher and the university, the copy shop's actions violated copyright law. Furthermore, said the court, the copy shop's actions violated all four tests for fair use (see *SA 2d*, p. 676). Characterizing the defendant's arguments as "sophistry," the court awarded summary judgment to the publishers.

* * * *

Colleges are increasingly turning to Internet-based services to detect plagiarism by students, at least in relation to writing a research paper. Turnitin.com is a popular service that compares a student's paper with other student papers in its database, as well as with journal articles and periodicals. If the school or college so wishes, the student's paper then becomes part of Turnitin's database, and is subsequently used for comparison with other student papers.

In *A.V. v. iParadigms*, LLC, 562 F.3d 630 (4th Cir. 2009), four high school students sued the parent company of Turnitin.com, arguing that the retention of their papers was a copyright violation. The company argued that its archiving of the student papers was "fair use." The court analyzed the use of the student papers under the four-part test for fair use. The court determined that (1) the use was "transformative" in that it was using the papers for something other than communicating information and ideas; (2) the company was not "publishing the papers," but merely comparing them with other documents; (3) despite the fact that the company was using the students' papers in their entirety, that fact did not preclude a finding of fair use because of the "transformative" use of the papers; and (4) the company's use of the papers did not harm the market for them because the company did not share the papers with others. The court affirmed the lower court's award of summary judgment to iParadigms.

****

The Higher Education Opportunity Act, passed in 2008, contains language related to institutions' responsibilities vis-à-vis illegal peer-to-peer file sharing. The U.S. Department of Education issued a final rule (*74 Fed. Reg.* 55910 (Oct. 29, 2009)) that adopts in full the proposed rule issued in August of 2009 (74 *Fed. Reg.* 42391 (Aug. 21, 2009)). The new rule requires the institution to agree that it has "developed and implemented written plans to effectively combat the unauthorized distribution of copyrighted material by users of the institution's network without unduly interfering with the educational and research use of the network." The plan must include technology-based deterrents, mechanisms for educating students and staff about appropriate and inappropriate use of copyrighted material, procedures for handling unauthorized distribution of copyrighted material, including disciplinary procedures, and "procedures for periodically reviewing the effectiveness of the plans to combat the unauthorized distribution of copyrighted materials. . .using relevant assessment criteria." The regulations leave it up to each institution to determine what assessment criteria it will use.

The U.S. Department of Education has issued a "Dear Colleague" letter that provides a sample summary of penalties, both civil and criminal, for copyright infringement. Institutions may use this sample letter to meet the requirement of the regulations that the institution include such a summary in information that it provides to prospective and current students. The Dear Colleague letter is available at http://www.ifap.ed.gov/dpcletters/GEN1008.html.

Sec. 14.5. Americans with Disabilities Act

A federal trial court has ruled that a public university is not protected by sovereign immunity when sued under Title II of the ADA. In *Goonewardena v. State of New York,* 475 F. Supp. 2d 310 (S.D.N.Y. 2007), a student at Hunter College had been suspended for stalking, harassing, and physically assaulting another student. When the college would not let the student return, he sued the college under Title II of the ADA, among other claims.

The college argued that the student's claims were barred by sovereign immunity, and moved to dismiss the claims. The court used a test articulated in *United States v. Georgia,* 546 U.S. 151 (2006), in which the Court stated that "insofar as Title II creates a private cause of action for damages against the States for conduct that *actually* violates the Fourteenth Amendment, Title II validly abrogates state sovereign immunity" (546 U.S. 151, 159). The test requires a court to determine "on a claim-by-claim basis, (1) which aspects of the State's alleged conduct violated Title II; (2) to what extent such misconduct also violated the Fourteenth Amendment; and (3) insofar as such misconduct violated Title II but did not violate the Fourteenth Amendment, whether Congress's purported abrogation of sovereign immunity as to that class of conduct is nevertheless valid" (546 U.S. 151, 159). The trial court determined that the plaintiff had stated a claim of a Title II violation; that the plaintiff's allegations had not stated a Fourteenth Amendment violation; but that Congress validly abrogated sovereign immunity because of the history of exclusion of students with disabilities from education. The court also noted that four federal circuit courts have concluded that Title II claims against public colleges and universities are not precluded by sovereign immunity: *Assn. for Disabled Americans v. Florida Int'l Univ.,* 405 F.3d 954, 959 (11th Cir. 2005); *Constantine v. Rectors and Visitors of George Mason University,* 411 F.3d 474, 490 (4th Cir. 2005); *Toledo v. Sanchez,* 454 F.3d 24, 40 (1st Cir. 2006); *Bowers v. NCAA,* 475 F.3d 524 (3d Cir. 2007); and *Phiffer v. Columbia River Corr. Inst.,* 384 F.3d 791 (9th Cir. 2004).

Sec. 14.9. Civil Rights Compliance

14.9.1. General considerations. Civil rights laws passed under the Constitution's Spending Clause (see *SA 2d,* p. 725) create an administrative enforcement process and, in some cases, a private right of action against the recipient of the federal funds (the college or university). The laws do not, however, provide that an aggrieved person can sue the federal agency that enforces a particular civil rights law if the individual is unhappy with the agency's enforcement process (or its decision not to proceed against the funding recipient). For example, in *Sherman v. Black,* 2009 U.S. App. LEXIS 5635 (2d Cir. 3/17/2009) (unpublished), Sherman, who had been dismissed from SUNY Downstate Medical Center on academic grounds, filed a disability discrimination complaint against the medical school with the U.S. Office for

Civil Rights (OCR). OCR concluded that the dismissal had been for legitimate, nondiscriminatory reasons, and rejected Sherman's appeal and request for reconsideration. Sherman then attempted to sue the U.S. Department of Education, asking the court to order OCR to conduct "conflict resolution" proceedings that would culminate in his readmission to the medical school. Citing *Women's Equity Action League v. Cavazos* (see *SA 2d*, p.727), the court ruled that Sherman did not have a cause of action against OCR, but must sue the medical school for disability discrimination under Section 504. The court dismissed his claim for lack of subject matter jurisdiction.

* * * *

One "scope and coverage" issue (see *SA 2d*, p. 726), concerning the "extraterritorial" application of the civil rights spending statutes, is increasing in importance due to the globalization of higher education. The issue concerns whether, and if so when, these statutes apply to acts allegedly violating the statute when those acts take place in a foreign country. See generally Arlene Kanter, "The Presumption Against Extraterritoriality as Applied to Disability Discrimination Laws: Where Does It Leave Students with Disabilities Studying Abroad?" 14 *Stanford L. & Pol'y Rev.* 291 (2003). In *Phillips v. St. George's University*, 2007 WL 3407728, 2007 U.S. Dist. LEXIS 84674 (E.D.N.Y. 2007), for example, the court refused to apply Title IX to alleged sexual harassment of a student while she was attending a university in Grenada. In an earlier case, however, *King v. Board of Control of Eastern Michigan University*, 221 F. Supp. 2d 783 (E.D. Mich. 2002), the court did apply Title IX to the alleged sexual harassment of students while they were in South Africa participating in a study abroad program sponsored by their home university in the United States. The court in the *Phillips* case distinguished *King* on grounds that the students in *King* were on a five-week study abroad program that was under control of the students' "home" university in the United States.

14.9.3. Title IX. In *Fitzgerald v. Barnstable School Committee*, 129 S. Ct. 788 (2009), the U.S. Supreme Court confirmed that Title IX does not subsume or preclude Section 1983 claims challenging the same discriminatory conduct as the Title IX claim (see *SA 2d*, pp. 737–38). The plaintiffs had sued a local school board and the superintendent of schools, alleging that their response to peer sexual harassment violated both Title IX and Section 1983. Allowing the suit to proceed, a unanimous Court determined that "Title IX was not meant to be an exclusive mechanism for addressing gender discrimination in schools, or a substitute for §1983 suits as a means of enforcing constitutional [equal protection] rights"; and that "Congress intended Title IX to be interpreted . . . to allow for parallel and concurrent §1983 claims" (129 S. Ct. at 797).

The *Barnstable School Committee* case also confirmed that Title IX, unlike Section 1983, imposes liability only on institutions and not on their officers and employees (see *SA 2d*, p.737). According to the Court, Title IX "has consistently been interpreted as not authorizing suit against school officials, teachers, and other individuals" (129 S. Ct. at 796). This statement apparently precludes Title IX suits against individuals in both their official and individual capacities— in which case the defendant superintendent in *Barnstable School Committee* could be sued only under Section 1983, whereas the school district could be sued under both Title IX and Section 1983.

15

Private Entities

Sec. 15.2. Accrediting Agencies

Another major accreditation issue that has been prominent since the beginning of the twenty-first century (see *SA 2d*, p. 762) concerns "accountability." The focus has been on accrediting agencies' accountability to students, parents, and the general public, particularly with respect to student achievement, and on the role of the U.S. Department of Education in overseeing an enhancement of accrediting agencies' accountability. In the Higher Education Opportunity Act of 2008 (HEOA), P.L. No. 110–315, 122 Stat. 3078, Congress addressed various aspects of accrediting agency accountability, as well as other issues concerning accreditation. The overall result, it appears, is to expand the federal government's role in accreditation and particularly in accrediting agency accountability. Critics have argued that the new accreditation provisions in HEOA, and the Department of Education's regulations and guidelines that implement these provisions, will result in federal government involvement in certain academic judgments of institutions, thus eroding institutional autonomy; and will push accreditation away from its traditional role as a voluntary process of peer and professional review toward a new role of monitoring institutional compliance with federal government priorities. See, for example, Judith Eaton, "Accreditation and the Federal Future of Higher Education," *Academe* (Sept./Oct. 2010), pp. 21–24. (Judith Eaton is the president of the Council for Higher Education Accreditation [CHEA]; see *SA 2d*, p. 760.)

Sec. 15.3. Athletic Associations and Conferences

15.3.2. Federal constitutional constraints. *Cohane v. National Collegiate Athletic Association*, 2007 WL 247710 (2d Cir. 2007), illustrates another type of state action claim that may still be open to plaintiffs after the U.S. Supreme Court's decision in *Tarkanian* (*SA 2d*, pp. 764–65). In *Cohane*, a basketball coach alleged that he was forced to resign after the NCAA issued a report about his program. The U.S. district court, relying on *Tarkanian*, had dismissed the case because the allegations in the coach's complaint, even if proven, would not constitute state action. The appellate court, distinguishing *Tarkanian*, reversed the district court. According to the appellate court, the coach's allegations about willful joint action between the university and the NCAA (see example on *SA 2d*, p. 766) and about improprieties in the university's cooperation with the NCAA, if proven, could constitute state action on the NCAA's part.

15.3.4. Antitrust laws. As a recent case illustrates, antitrust issues can also involve athletic associations' "play and equipment" rules, in which case the complainants may be manufacturers or distributors of athletic equipment. In *Warrior Sports, Inc. v. National Collegiate Athletic Association*, 623 F.3d 281 (6th Cir. 2010), a manufacturer and distributor of lacrosse sticks challenged the NCAA's revision of a "rule that governs the size of lacrosse stickheads approved for use in NCAA-sanctioned play." After the district court rejected the plaintiff's claim based on the pleadings, the appellate court affirmed. It assumed, without deciding, that the NCAA's enforcement of its rule was a commercial activity subject to section 1 of the Sherman Act, but then held that, under the rule-of-reason approach (see *SA 2d*, pp. 769–71), "the challenged rule does not harm competition and, consequently, does not unreasonably restrain trade or commerce."

Case Index

Statute Index

Subject Index